IRREPLACEABLE YOU

BRAVELY LIVING IN THE SKIN YOU'RE IN

J. K. Olson

WORTHY*
Inspired

Published by Worthy Inspired, an imprint of Worthy Publishing Group, a division of Worthy Media, Inc., One Franklin Park, 6100 Tower Circle, Suite 210, Franklin, TN 37067.

WORTHY is a registered trademark of Worthy Media, Inc.

HELPING PEOPLE EXPERIENCE THE HEART OF GOD

eBook available wherever digital books are sold.

Library of Congress Cataloging-in-Publication Data
Names: Olson, J. K., author.
Title: Irreplaceable you : bravely living in the skin you're in / by J.K.
   Olson.
Description: Franklin, TN : Worthy Publishing, 2017.
Identifiers: LCCN 2017005509 | ISBN 9781683970316 (hardcover)
Subjects: LCSH: Self-esteem--Religious aspects--Christianity--Meditations.
Classification: LCC BV4598.24 .O57 2017 | DDC 242--dc23
LC record available at https://lccn.loc.gov/2017005509

Printed in the United States of America
17 18 19 20 21 LBM 10 9 8 7 6 5 4 3 2 1

Thanks to Marilyn,
for the New Year's Eve Edna Mode pep talk,
and to Tarisa and Willa,
for vital first reader feedback.

And to my husband, ,
who, in the months when I was writing this,
when I would anxiously wring my hands and say,
"I need to get a job,"
would calmly say, "You have one."
Thank you.

Lord, help us to live a life of speaking what's true.
Thank you that our brokenness
is a greater bridge to other people
than pretending to be whole ever is.

SHEILA WALSH

INTRODUCTION

Growing up, I always thought that money spent on some-one else's words was worth more than food, clothes, or even a new BB gun. Reading and breathing seemed about the same in importance, with only one filled with ideas and new experiences. And I really wanted to go places besides the hayloft.

Now, decades later, I find I haven't really gone as far geographically as I thought I would. But my words are on these pages, someone made them look really professional, and they will soon be in the hands of others. I did not expect this in any daydream.

This book came as a result of five very difficult years, including four funerals, all suicides. It made me desper-ate to not let one opportunity pass to show others their unique strength and beauty. To reflect the value and love God has for us, even as we are frantically kneeling in front of our own self-destruction.

I see that in myself. And in writing this, I was reminded, and could see more clearly, the love relationship He pursues with me. With you. So thank you.

Who we are, including all of our ugly backstory, is a one-of-a-kind message of His transformation waiting to be told.

ACCEPTED

O LORD, you have searched me [thoroughly]
and have known me. . . .
You understand my thought from afar.

PSALM 139:1–2 AMP

I was at college in Chicago when I received a letter from my mother that mentioned my sister had prayed with a friend to receive Jesus. I was glad to hear it, but as I walked down La Salle Street on my way to work, comparison reared its ugly head: I have never prayed with one of my friends. Here I am, going to Bible college. I felt like a hypocrite. A failure, even.

My sister and I always have been more different than alike. I've had six inches and fifty pounds on her since birth, practically. She is social, I am not. She went through a Pat Benatar stage, I liked Bing Crosby. (I remember this only because of the Bing Crosby's Greatest Hits album that she bought for me in high school. I think she bought me that album because I did not want to change the radio station in the car when Bing came on. Did I like the song just because she didn't? A strong possibility.)

But our differences didn't matter. Did Jesus say, "Go ye extroverts into all the world . . ."? No.

When I reached the door of the drug rehabilitation center where I worked, I stood and held the door open for Regina, one of our clients, who was coming down the sidewalk with her shopping cart.

She stopped halfway through the door and looked at me. "Are you a Christian?" she asked quietly.

I was surprised, but even more so by her reply when I said yes.

"I can feel the love of God coming from you." She looked at me intently for a few seconds, then continued in.

Something that I had known in my head moved to my heart: God saw me. He used a homeless woman like an angelic messenger in the exact moment of my self-accusation to tell me I was accepted, loved, and could be used by Him.

Father, thank You for the priceless timing of Your message
of value to me all those years ago.
Thank You for never comparing Your daughters
or wanting us to be more like one another.
Thank You for my sister's strengths, thank You for mine,
and thank You so much for the tender way
You care for each of us.

GRACE-GIVERS, TRUTH-TELLERS, STANDARD-BEARERS

Let His banner over me be love.

SONG OF SONGS 2:4 NIV

When I was in high school, I asked a teacher if he would fill out a college reference form for me. He did, and gave it back to me to mail. He said very positive things, one that I remember still: *Jill can do anything she puts her mind to.* I was humbled and amazed that he saw that in me. Many times in the years that followed, I thought about that. Sometimes not believing, but never knocking it down. I came back to it often.

Our words have the power to breathe truth into others. They can be a lasting gift, a mirror, reflecting what someone has lost sight of in themselves, or maybe has never seen at all.

When the Israelites were walking through the wilderness to their land of promise, they carried banners that identified each tribe. After centuries of slavery, it served, among other things, as a visual reminder of who they were: God's chosen. God had made that clear to their forefather:

> Your name is Jacob, but you will no longer be called Jacob; your name will be Israel. . . . A nation and a community of nations will come from you, and kings will be among your descendants. The land I gave to Abraham and Isaac I also give to you, and I will give this land to your descendants after you (Genesis 35:10–12 NIV).

The banners proclaimed the truth of their identity, the names of the tribes, Jacob's twelve sons, as they journeyed toward their promised land.

Armies at the time also used banners, which identified rallying points before battle. The Bible gives us a rare glimpse of the important position of those who held up the banners, also called *standards*. Isaiah 10:18 says when the standard-bearer faints, the nation's glory fades away (KJV). The identity and rallying points are gone.

I want to be that standard-bearer. As those around me battle for victory day after day, I want my words to brand them with truth about who God says they are: people who are loved by Him, honored by Him. I want to marshal them to the purpose God has written in their names, to the identity planned before they were born.

Let's hold high a banner of love by revealing the beauty of people, by speaking kind and encouraging words to them, always keep those words of truth in plain sight. That banner of truth may be the very thing that keeps them going.

Father, thank You for the power of our words over others.
Help us to speak truth about the incredible love
You have for them.

PURSUED

The Son of Man has come to seek
and to save that which was lost.

LUKE 19:10 NASB

We all make bad decisions at times. But even in the midst of wrong choices, God says, "I'm not leaving you. You're mine" (1 Samuel 12:20–22, paraphrase). It was a life-changing surprise to me, during a time when I knew I was experiencing God's discipline (the painful consequences of my own actions), to feel that He was closer than ever. It was like He pulled me into His lap right in the midst of my despair to whisper His gentle acceptance and continued love.

Jesus's acceptance of Zacchaeus was life-changing for him too.

Zacchaeus takes up a mere ten verses in just one Gospel, but his creative approach to Jesus is well remembered. He wanted to see who Jesus was, but couldn't because of the crowd surrounding Him, so Zacchaeus ran down the path ahead of everyone and climbed a tree.

Imagine Zacchaeus's surprise when Jesus stopped near the tree, looked up, and spoke to him by name. "Zaccheus, hurry and come down, for today I must stay at your house" (Luke 19:5 NASB).

Jesus didn't tell Zacchaeus He might stay at his house or even that he would like to stay at his house. It appears Jesus's time with Zacchaeus was written long before that sycamore started to grow.

Jesus interacted with people in a lot of different ways, but this is the only time we see Him inviting Himself over to someone's house. Jesus showed a fondness for this man whose sin was so very public, and the man was more than giddy.

Zacchaeus quickly climbed down and took Jesus to his house in great excitement and joy. But the people were displeased. "He has gone to be the guest of a notorious sinner," they grumbled.

Meanwhile, Zacchaeus stood before the Lord

and said, "I will give half my wealth to the poor, Lord, and if I have cheated people on their taxes, I will give them back four times as much" (Luke 19:6–8 NLT).

Jesus doesn't hold back in disgust at our sin. We encounter Him right there *in the middle* of our own way, and find Him loving us unconditionally. And we are never the same.

Jesus, thank You for Your love that pursues us,
even in the pain of our own mistakes.
Thank You that a time-out away from You
is never part of Your plan.

YES. WHAT ELSE?

Casting all your cares [all your anxieties, all your worries,
and all your concerns, once and for all] on Him,
for He cares about you [with deepest affection,
and watches over you very carefully].

1 PETER 5:7 AMP

A family friend of ours was a paratrooper with the 101st Airborne Division during WWII whose unit parachuted into Normandy in the dark. A few months before he died, I asked him what he thought about being called the Greatest Generation. He was quiet before he responded. "I don't know if we were great as much as we were hearty," he said. So both.

There are times when it doesn't matter much what is going on inside you, you just have to push forward no matter what. Emotions can be seen as things that need to be overcome.

But for many of us, this push forward no matter what, or "buck up" mentality, is a way of life, inherited from generations of those who associate it with survival. We can mistakenly see God like that, as someone who has His foot on our backs to push us out of the plane, rather than One who picks us up and jumps with us.

There was a time when I had more anger and anxiety than I could handle. I asked God to take it from me regularly, but victory was always short-lived. One day, I just started typing furiously, describing to God in detail what I was feeling, the darkest and ugliest I had.

Instead of feeding the fire or feeling like trash, with all of it staring at me in black and white, I was surprised by the feeling that this was exactly what I should be doing. It was almost like God was coaxing me on, responding to every admission with, *Yes. What else?* I learned that my anger was a response to something more that God couldn't address with me until I took the time to present it to Him in detail. I needed to walk into the details with Him before I could let it go.

In the verse above, Peter could have said, "Why are you concerning yourself with those cares? Don't you realize how powerful God is?" Instead, he shows us the heart of God and gives us the how-to: cast all your cares on Him, for He cares about you.

If we try to just buck up and push forward, we're denying the intimate relationship and restoration He desires for us. In His gentleness and respect for our choice, as cliché as it sounds, He will only take what we give Him.

Thank You, God, that there is not a place we can go,
inside or out, where You aren't there,
waiting for us to come to You.

WHY DO YOU CALL ME GOOD?

A man ran up to Him and knelt before Him, and asked Him,
"Good Teacher, what shall I do to inherit eternal life?"
And Jesus said to him, "Why do you call Me good?
No one is good except God alone.

MARK 10:17–18 NASB

For many years this response from Jesus confused me. Why in the world would He question His own goodness? It seemed like He was being a witness for His own prosecution. I could just hear the Pharisees' courtroom-like accusations: "And wasn't it you yourself who questioned why you were being called good because God alone is good?"

One day, I determined to be the persistent widow and continue asking until He gave me clarity. I asked for wisdom, battering again and again: "Lord, I don't understand. Why would you question someone calling You good? You invented good. Will you give me an understanding beyond my own here? Jesus, please show me why You said this."

I don't know how long I was at it, repeating versions of the same request, before I understood the answer. It dropped into my mind and I praised Him for it, at the same time feeling like the last one aboard the USS Common Knowledge.

Jesus was asking a leading question. He really wanted the man to think about what he was saying and draw the conclusions himself.

Jesus continued to lead him. Instead of mentioning that whoever believes in Him has eternal life, as He had said to Nicodemus, Jesus listed six commandments—ones He knew this man had kept. And when the ruler replied, "Teacher, I have kept these from my youth up," the Gospel of Mark records that Jesus felt love for him.

This man wasn't attempting to prove his own goodness. He was kneeling before Jesus, sincerely seeking. Jesus's response showed him that he'd gone as far as he could in his own efforts. "One thing you lack: go and sell all you possess and give to the poor, and you will have treasure in heaven; and come, follow Me."

Jesus's response was like a mirror, revealing the man's own heart to himself, and he walked away grieved. Then in the following verse Jesus gave the remaining crowd an unforgettable word picture: "[I]t is easier for a camel to go through the eye of a needle than for a rich man to enter the kingdom of God." Their astonished "Who then can be saved?" prompted the beautiful answer of a loving God to our inability: "All things are possible with God."

Jesus sees our hearts and speaks to us as individuals. He gave Nicodemus one answer, and this rich young man another, connecting directly, intimately with the thoughts and intensions of each. And when this rich, young ruler walked away, Jesus's unanswered question, and the key to his quest for eternal life, followed him: "Why do you call Me good? No one is good except God alone."

Jesus, thank You for how You communicate with us
so individually, so intimately. Help me to let go of anything
I am holding to more tightly than I hold onto You,
even my own efforts.

HIS TENDER TIMING

For everything there is a season, a time for every activity under heaven. A time to be born and a time to die.

ECCLESIASTES 3:1–2 NLT

Toward the end of her life, a series of strokes took my grandmother's ability to speak and move. One night as I sat reading to her, I told her she needed to hold on long enough to meet my first child. She didn't make eye contact much at that point, but her blue eyes turned and locked on mine. I knew she had something to say but no way to communicate it. She died soon after, the same month I conceived our first child.

The same year I miscarried our first child.

My baby was here, and then she was gone. It may not make sense, but I craved to know who was caring for her now. Then I had a dream, a short vision of my grandmother, sitting in her rocker, holding my baby. I couldn't approach them, and I couldn't see my baby's face, but I could see my grandmother's full, tender attention on my "little lambie," as she called her grandchildren. My sister had a similar dream after her miscarriage.

The next year, when I was pregnant again, my husband's job took us out of state. We moved away from all family and into an apartment complex that had so many senior citizens, the locals thought it was an old folks' home.

Less than two years after moving in, we had two beautiful, healthy boys. To get out of the house, I often took them down with me to the community room for morning coffee.

The ladies around that table were shameless in the attention they gave the boys, and in their attempts to feed my babies sugar. One morning, I jokingly asked if they had anything to talk about when we weren't there. Viv, a spunky eighty-something widow who had taken it upon herself to keep my door decorated according to season, replied, "Oh yes, we say, 'I wonder what the boys are up to now?'"

At my boys' first birthday parties, the ladies wore hats,

gave gifts, and shared cupcakes. When I was trying to clean off my son's place at the table, Lola smiled from the chair next to us and said quietly, "Don't mind the crumbs, Jill, there'll be plenty more of those." A comforting perspective from someone who had seen generations of temporary concerns. A perspective my grandmother would have had. And when Lola sang, her sweet soprano voice lifted happy birthday wishes to the ceiling and brought tears to my eyes. The room was a choir full of my grandmother's voice.

Lord, thank You for Your love that orchestrates
how you bring people in even as others have to leave.
Thank You for the blessing of loved ones we have known
for a very short time, and of those who have shaped our lives.
Thank You for the care You give to that ushering in and out,
oftentimes in ways we don't even see.

CHASING THE TAXFISH

Go to the sea and throw in a hook, and take the first fish that comes up; and when you open its mouth, you will find a shekel. Take that and give it to them for you and Me.

MATTHEW 17:27 NASB

Jesus could have come up with that shekel for their taxes a million different ways. He could have just pulled it out of His pocket, out of Peter's pocket, or out of Peter's ear. But in His infinite intention and wisdom, He sent Peter fishing.

Peter seems like the kind of guy who tried to take things into his own hands (like a sword in a garden). This may be a characteristic of the life-form called *human*. It describes me, for sure.

I see Peter heading out confidently to the water to find the fish. Did he get in a boat and head back to the spot where he had been fishing when Jesus called him? To the place where Jesus had instructed them to go back out, and with one throw of the net they brought in enough fish to overflow two boats? I can picture Peter dropping a hook there, at the seaside memorial of God's goodness. Surely that's where the taxfish would be.

When nothing bites, Peter changes poles. Then baits. Still nothing. He scans the surface of the water. Did the fish swallow a shekel that fell from a fisherman's pocket, near shore? Maybe he needed a metal detector.

I imagine that is when it hits him. Jesus's words were simple: throw in a hook, take the first fish that comes up. Peter realizes that Jesus didn't send him because he knew how to fish. The minute he understands that, he leans back and feels a tug on the line.

We know that Jesus knew what people were doing who were outside of His own human vision (John 1:48). I expect He was aware of the whole scene, amused, then delighted when Peter finally figured it out. I believe His delight is also with us when we have faith enough to rely fully on Him to bring about the good things He desires for us when we're following His will.

L. B. Cowman said, "Only God Himself, who always works without straining, and who never overworks, can do the work He assigns to His children." It's His to accomplish, ours to trust.

What a beautiful thing.

Jesus, thank You that we can relax and trust You.
Show us when we start stressing by trusting
in our own ability. Help us to trust You to show us
what our own "throw in a hook" looks like.

FAMILY TREE

For you have not received a spirit of slavery leading
to fear again, but you have received a spirit of adoption
as sons by which we cry out, "Abba! Father!"
ROMANS 8:15 NASB

A few years ago, my sister helped her high schooler sift through information that they requested "from the four corners of the earth" for an assignment to create a family tree. Her words about it are a hopeful reminder to families like ours, familiar with addiction and abuse.

I find myself on a sentimental journey over a people I have never even met and yet we are bound together by blood. It strikes me that without them, there is no us, and I am compelled to know more as patterns become visible from generation to generation, not all righteous or desired. The branches of a family can hold many secrets, some ugly and pain ridden. No generational line is without the stain of sin which causes our "tree" to be twisted and diseased. It began in the Garden of Eden when we believed a lie and ate from the wrong tree, multiplying the effects of the wrong tree for the generations to come. . . . But there is a happy ending! A new Seed has been released to the earth, without blemish, that will cleanse us and graft us into a new heritage, a birthright of righteousness through faith in the Redemptive Seed. This Seed is Love incarnate . . . Jesus Christ of Nazareth.

When we confess our need for forgiveness and issue Him a take-all-of-me invitation, we become not just slicked up, pothole-healed versions of yesterday, but of a new seed entirely. "Anyone who belongs to Christ has become a new person. The old life is gone; the new life has begun!" (2 Corinthians 5:17 NLT).

The spirit of adoption that He gives cries out *Abba,* Father! in us in ways we can't even understand, connecting us with Him for a new heritage of hope. A hope that holds beyond our circumstances when we fill ourselves with His Word and spend time in His presence.

The effects of addiction and other dysfunction can follow a family line beyond the generation in which it happened. Jesus continues to redeem as we live in a close, honest relationship with Him, letting His love shake out any hurts that we hold closer to our hearts than Him. We can trust Him to do that tenderly.

My sister's high schooler is now graduated and the family tree assignment boxed, but not forgotten. Who we come from remains a part of us, and we're thankful to know their unique struggles and sacrifices as we live out the miracle of new life in Christ.

Jesus, thank You for the family You have given us.
As Nehemiah and Daniel prayed for forgiveness for the nation
of Israel, I ask Your forgiveness for the sins of our family.
Let the forgiveness offered through Your Son become a part
of our redeemed heritage. Thank You for Your promise
of goodness that fills tomorrow.

NEW STRENGTH

Because the Lord is my Shepherd, I have everything I need!
He lets me rest in the meadow grass and leads me
beside the quiet streams. He gives me new strength.
He helps me do what honors him the most.

PSALM 23: 1–3 TLB

I was feeling like a failure in teaching my children the prime directive Jesus had given: love God and love others. Two of my children could not be in the same room without fighting, despite all my efforts to help promote at least friendship between them.

So I prayed. Helpless. And went to bed, a failure. The next day, things were different. I had a new patience and love for my children. Instead of every fight or exchange feeling like sandpaper, I was able to address the issue calmly. I also had opportunities throughout the day to talk to my kids one-on-one, without even seeking them out. And I was able to really listen to them.

It is so easy to feel like I am on top of things when circumstances are going well, when no fights are breaking out. And I lose sight of Him being the curator, the ultimate caretaker and lover of the hearts of my children.

How long will it take before I can make a habit of praying through all circumstances pertaining to my children? (For some people it is their finances, or their self-worth, or their future.) Even though the issue continues to rise up, so does the ever-present help in need that God gives. I never feel the door closing, as if God is disgusted, saying, "Well, if you don't have this down by now. . . ." That frustration comes from inside me. Inside us.

He is the shepherd of my heart, as well as my children's. And yours.

A lot of our anxiety comes from a fear of what *could* happen, or of what our children are becoming, doesn't it? I want to walk and lead my kids down a path of love for God that will guide them as they grow up and move away. But in the end, I am not the one behind that curtain. God is the one in control.

I am just someone who believes in the love and power of God, but who sometimes lets other things fog my awareness. Just one mom who wakes up to find His gentle, shepherding presence has come in unexpectedly to show me that He is at work in ways beyond what I can accomplish, or dream of accomplishing.

He doesn't leave yesterday's mercies here because we obviously somehow missed them when they were fresh. He gives them brand-new every single day, to each of us.

Jesus, thank You for being with me in the trenches of my day. Teach me more about abiding in You.

BLESSED REFLECTION

Hope in God, for I shall again praise Him
for the help of His presence.

PSALM 42:5 NASB

It was an excruciating morning, trying to get the boys to clean their bedrooms so we could then get to Walmart. I would leave one boy in one room to help another in the next, only to go back to the first room and find nothing had been done while I was gone. I was borderline raving lunatic when all was said and done.

I asked them to give me quiet time in my room. I yelled at them a few times from the inside when it got too noisy. I prayed for insight, then journaled:

- Plan better.
- Show them step by step.
- Give them control.

I so wanted that last one—to be an example of someone in control, not frustrated.

We made it to Walmart. We picked up three things in the grocery section, then headed for the feminine items on the other side of the store. When we got there, my youngest said he didn't feel good. I grabbed what I needed as he was saying he thinks he is going to throw up. We came up to the checkouts at Mach speed.

He threw up as I was taking him out of the cart. Not a little. The other boys scattered: one to a bench by the bathrooms, facing away; the other, his face buried in a box of candy or gum a few aisles over. I wiped my little guy's mouth with my gloves. I heard someone in jewelry say she was glad she wasn't on clean-up today. He hurled again.

We left the cart and went home. Later, lying next to my precious child who slept while I stroked his hair, I realized I felt content. Satisfied to be able to care for my child when he was sick. A great change from how I felt that morning, like a mom unfit for face-to-face contact. In that moment, it seemed like a message from God. He was showing me a reflection of myself that I couldn't see that day.

He sees us. Not just the raving lunatic mom, the angry

child, the flunking student, the relapsed addict, the failed businessman, or the sinner, but the caring mom, the loving son or daughter, the hurting teen, the confused, and the flawed-but-trying.

And He is there, ministering to each individual, giving powerful, living hope for a better tomorrow.

Jesus, thank You for how you change situations that feel so despairing and unchangeable, often in a shorter time than we think possible. Thank You for the hope You bring, and for caring about how we see ourselves.

You care about our self-image.

Thank You for helping me understand that.

CONSTRUCTION ZONE

Humility goes before honor.

PROVERBS 18:12 NASB

Not long enough ago, I screeched to a stop in my Camry and had words with a road construction worker. My teenage son pressed himself as flat as possible against his seat as we "talked" across him. The worker's face was red and I could see his bottom teeth as he yelled. He ended by saying that a worker was recently hit and killed by a driver.

I was sorry about that, I replied quietly. Then maintained that I was slowing down, and I did not almost hit one of his workers.

It wouldn't have helped had I told him that the brakes

were going on the car, and I was slowing down as fast as I could. That my husband had lost his job, and we were losing our house, but soon we would replace those brakes. I had stood up on the brakes, tires screeching, to come to a stop when I saw him throw his hat on the road in anger. I'm not sure why I stopped.

Maybe because I was doing all I could, but it wasn't enough.

"I wasn't yelling, just trying to be heard," I told my son on the way home.

"You were yelling," he said.

As soon as we were home, I went to my room feeling so unsettled and anxious, I begged God to speak to me. Then I opened my Bible "randomly" to Exodus 8.

Pharaoh was asking Moses to plead with the Lord to take the plague of frogs away. Moses's reply to Pharaoh in verse nine stopped me. He says:

> "The honor is yours to tell me: when shall I entreat for you and your servants and your people, that the frogs be destroyed from you and your houses, that they may be left only in the Nile?" (NASB)

The words came off the page: "The honor is yours. . . ." Pharaoh was far from perfect. He was enslaving, abusing Moses's people. Yet Moses was careful to honor him

I was so relieved to have something to confess. I went to my knees and repented for my lack of honor toward the worker. I asked God to bless him and keep him and the crew safe. And then I told my son that I was wrong, I shouldn't have acted that way. He calmly agreed.

Later, I felt God impress on me: You honor people because of who you are, not because of who they are.

In those still small words, I felt His honor toward me.

Thank You, Jesus, for Your forgiveness,
and for the foundation of Your love that defines me,
directs me, and is slowly, certainly, transforming me.

A PASTOR AND A HIPPIE

With all the earnestness I possess I tell you this:
Unless you are born again,
you can never get into the Kingdom of God.

JOHN 3:3 TLB

I always thought my family's earliest encounter with Jesus started out like a joke: a pastor and a hippie walk into a bar. After talking to my formerly long-haired uncle, I realized that part didn't come until later.

Our family's introduction to Jesus really started in the early 1970s after a pastor asked his congregation a question: What would they do if a group of dirty hippies walked through the door of their church?

Can you guess who came to church the next Sunday? One of them was my uncle. He had been invited personally by Pastor P.

Almost fifty years later, he remembers the multitude of invitations to lunch that came after that service. "Did that interest you then, sharing a meal and rubbing shoulders with church-folk like that?" I asked. His response was immediate.

"Are you kidding me? Free food?"

When my uncle was saved, he went home and shared the Good News with his family. We were there, and my mother remembers discussing it with her father as they washed the dishes. "It didn't even make sense to us, that you didn't have to earn salvation," she told me.

Meanwhile (don't you love how history is filled with God's "meanwhiles"—His orchestration of circumstances that are all working their way together toward their assigned place in His timing?), meanwhile, a neighbor lady was persistently inviting my mother to church.

Mom had no desire to go, so she did the only neighborly thing she could think of. She hid. She made excuses. But the day came when we all piled into the neighbor's car and went to church. Can you guess whose church it was?

Eventually, my parents both started attending hippie-loving Pastor P's church and came to know Jesus personally.

We rocked out when my uncles led music with their guitars at Vacation Bible School.

My uncles are now grandfathers. Because of Pastor P's willingness to reach those outside the walls of his church and his generation, which included going into bars with his new converts, Jesus continues to save and change lives in our family, down to the second and third generations and counting.

Thank You, Jesus, for the willingness of Pastor P.
Please bless him and pastors like him. Give us all direction
and courage to reach out to others with Your love,
especially to those whose lifestyles
are so different from ours.

PREMEDITATED

*You have tried my heart; You have visited **me** by night;*
You have tested me and You find nothing;
I have purposed that my mouth will not transgress.

PSALM 17:3 NASB

Social media has done great things for birthdays. Who isn't touched when so many people, many of whom we don't see regularly, take a few minutes to send us happiness on our day? It is a small picture of the power of our words to lift others up.

Of course, our words can also do great damage. I once overheard my twelve-year-old niece's friend whisper, "Quit talking" to my niece as she was engaged in conversation with someone else. I don't remember what she was talking about, just the comment. Because I immediately wished I had a friend like that! Someone who could gently warn me to shut my mouth.

In Psalm 17, David *predetermined* that he would not sin with his words. Often, hurtful words are given no forethought whatsoever and can last forever in someone's mind. Like David, we can write prayers of predetermination for words that build, instead.

Father, help my every reaction with others reflect the value and delight You take in them. Let me never miss another opportunity to speak kindness and acceptance to someone whether they appear to need it or not. For the times when I've been more interested in making an impression or a joke, when I haven't taken the time to really listen and understand, forgive me. Show me how to honor others by being slow to speak, to be tuned in to what someone is really saying, beyond the meaning of their words.

Make me more like You when You were here, engaging people in conversation with questions, drawing them out. Forgive me for the times I've shut others down with a quick slap of my opinion. Give me wisdom on how and when to give my opinion. Help me to let go of any need to have the last word.

When I've let someone's external appearance, facial expression, words spoken or not spoken lead me to believe something ugly about someone, forgive me. When I'm tempted to look at someone's flawed method of operating and feel like my reaction is justified, Jesus, remind me in Your gentle way that You are making all things new. You are restoring me, and You are also restoring the flawed operator.

Lord, when I'm reacting in my own issues and I'm not able to see someone else's hurt, give me the sense to come to You for wisdom, to rest on the identity You have given me, as holy in Your eyes and dearly loved. I will help other's see their precious place with You too.

Lord, give me eyes that I may see,
lest I, as people will, pass by someone's Calvary
and think it just a hill.
—Author unknown

LOVE UNHINGED

*The L*ORD *did not love you and choose you because you were*
*greater in number than any of the **other** peoples . . .*
*but because the L*ORD *loves you and is keeping*
the oath which He swore to your fathers.

DEUTERONOMY 7:7–8 AMP

It wasn't a good morning. I shut myself in my bedroom in
the middle of the day, tired and disgusted with myself. Why
was it that other mothers, who have more children than
I, are so much more even-keeled emotionally? What could
God do through me? With me? I climbed into bed, asked
God for help, and "randomly" flipped open my Bible to
Elijah and the showdown on Mount Carmel (1 Kings 18).

At that point in history, God's chosen nation had a king and queen who were enforcing idolatry. The queen had murdered the prophets of God, taken down His altars, and established Baal as the national deity. Under God's direction, Elijah issued invitations to the prophets of Baal for a divine competition. Each would cut up an ox and put it over wood. The god who answered by fire would be the winner.

Baal's prophets went first. After a whole day of listening to them plead in vain, at the time of the evening sacrifice, Elijah called everyone around with a simple, "Come here to me" (verse 30, NIV) While they watched, he cut the ox and doused the whole altar with water. Elijah prayed, "LORD, the God of Abraham, Isaac and Israel, today let it be known that You are God in Israel" (verse 36).

Immediately God answered with fire that consumed everything, even the water. When I read that, I wanted to fall down like the Israelites as they repeated, "The LORD— he is God! The LORD, he is God!" (verse 39).

Yet a few verses later this same prophet of God runs terrified to the wilderness. His prayer now is desperate: "Take my life, for I am no better than my ancestors" (19:4). Up one moment and defeated the next? A prophet of God?

But God, who had sent down all-consuming fire at Elijah's request, sets a table for him. There are no words between them. Just an angel dispatched, who gently wakes him to eat, twice, when all he wants to do is sleep. God is intimately aware of our weaknesses and provides us with every strength for what is ahead.

His love and plan for us is not hinged to our emotional perfection. He cares for us with a love that is hinged only to His own character: God is love.

Jesus, thank You for this timely example of Elijah.
Thank You for how You gently care for every part of us,
even our emotions, and for Your love
that does not need a reason.

TO SEE WHAT
HE WOULD NAME THEM

Out of the ground the LORD God formed every beast
of the field and every bird of the sky, and brought them
to the man to see what he would call them; and whatever
the man called a living creature, that was its name.

GENESIS 2:19 NASB

After one of my attempts at college, I worked full time for a friend at his new business. During lunch, we would have deep, theological discussions.

Him: When God first brought the animals to Adam in the garden, I believe the names he gave them were pet names.

Me: Pet names?

Him: Pet names. Rover.

Me (following pious reflection): Spot.

Him (after monkish meditation): Stripe.

Me (with theological pause): Longneck.

The vast majority of English translations of Genesis 2:19 (thank you, BibleGateway) say that God brought the animals to Adam "to see what he would name them." Not "so that he could name them." The action here is God seeing. His observation of the one created in His image.

It seems that God shared this characteristic with parents—a delight in observing how our children, so new to the world, react to everything they encounter and try to master. We like to keep record of their first words, great questions and responses. When my son was about two, I praised him lavishly when he first stood up like Dad to use the bathroom. He replied so seriously, "Mom, it's my finest hour." (A line from Larry the Cucumber, so brilliantly recalled, don't you think?) I wrote that down and told it more than once.

How do you think God reacted to Adam coming up with names in Genesis 2?

God: "And how about this one with his head way up in the leaves like that?"

He and Jesus wait with smiles.

Adam (cocking his head and puckering his eyebrows): "Big throat?"

God and Jesus laugh as they point to a book where an angel is already recording it.

I write this smiling because, while it is theologically anthropomorphic (I just pushed those two long words together all by myself! Exhausting.), it also seems just like Him. He could have just told Adam the names of the animals and, in His mercy, given him flashcards. But God desires to hear from us. Often His initial response, even when confronting sin, is to ask questions.

God, who created the universe in just a few days, who destroyed, protected, conquered, whom angels, powers, and authorities are subject to, is a Father God who dotes on you!

Father, thank You for Your delight in us.
Thank You for being the kind of God who waits
to hear from us and desires to be called Father.

STANDING?

*Trust in and rely confidently on the L*ORD *with all your heart
and do not rely on your own insight or understanding.
In all your ways know and acknowledge and recognize Him,
and He will make your paths straight and smooth
[removing obstacles that block your way].*

PROVERBS 3:5–6 AMP

For much of my life, I have doubted my ability to hear
from God. There have been a few times, however, when I
knew God had spoken directly to me.

Like the afternoon when, as a young parent, I felt I
couldn't love my boys like they deserved. And even when
I was able to "do it right," I wasn't able to maintain it. I felt

such despair as I cried out to God. Then 2 Thessalonians 3:5 came clearly into my mind. Just the reference. I paged through my Bible to find the verse. "May the Lord direct your hearts into the love of God and into the steadfastness of Christ" (AMP).

God saw me sitting on the couch that day. He heard and responded with such hope, addressing His ability to provide the love and steadfastness I sought.

But there are many times when I have talked myself out of the sureness, the quickening inside that I felt when reading specific Scripture. Do you know what I mean? It goes something like: *You are being led by your emotions again. "The heart is deceitful above all things" (Jeremiah 17:9). You are so desperate to hear God speak to this situation, you are talking for Him.*

For certain, there have been times when references came to my mind that didn't exist. Or times when I couldn't see the connection. The *me* part of it is imperfect. I am well aware of that. But because of the times when what I hear and feel is spot-on, I continue asking and listening.

During one hard season, when I felt shut off from hearing God, thinking my own dysfunction was standing in the way of my hearing from Him, the reference for 1 Corinthians 10:12 would not leave me. I looked it up, but didn't understand its significance: "Therefore let him who thinks he stands take heed that he does not fall" (NKJV).

I did not at all feel overconfident in my ability to stand. The opposite, if anything. It stayed on my mind, and I looked it up several times, wondering, asking God about it, until finally He addressed it with me. I was "standing" in my inability. I was giving more power to the dysfunction I felt than to Him, my mighty and powerful Savior.

In case you need to hear that, I'll confirm to you now: God is more powerful than any disability you feel. He pursues your trust, He pursues you.

Jesus, thank You for how You gently take our hands
to lead us out of the box we've put You in.
You are mighty and powerful and beyond words.
Thank You for Your intimate care for us,
and Your desire to lead us every day.

DILIGENT

But as for me, I trust in You, O LORD, I say,
"You are my God." My times are in Your hand.

PSALM 31:14–15 NASB

Have you ever prayed earnestly, heart-inside-out fervently, and nothing changed?

One night, thirty years after a fervent, unanswered prayer, I was thinking back on the situation, bringing it before God for the first time in a long time. In the quietness of my heart, I felt God say: *If I would have answered how you wanted, would you trust Me then?*

He asked so gently. It instantly revealed the conditional, circumstantial nature of my trust. It also showed me the heart of God. For the first time, I saw that He *pursued* my trust. In His hands-off, choice-honoring way.

Wasn't it trust that He was looking for with the Israelites in the desert? He had called them out to be a people called by His own name. He established a covenant with them, and provided for them. Manna, each morning, like a trail of bread crumbs leading to His faithfulness. Only, instead of a round belly and a trusting heart at the end of the trail, they only made it to the end of the trail. The fullness of trust wasn't there.

Over the years I hadn't stopped praying. I'd seen prayers answered, mine and those of others, and my trust had grown. But I had never come back to that one issue, never acknowledged my faith in Him as being Sovereign with the outcome of that. There was still a shadow of the teenage girl in me who had doubts about the goodness of God.

Finally, I was able to open my arms to Him. To entrust that long-ago wound to Him, and confess my belief in His faithfulness.

Our Savior will not leave any corner of us untouched, will He? He pursues every part, even what we think is no longer within reach. I am incredibly grateful.

When we're tempted to believe that things will never change, when our trust wavers and fear comes on strong, we can add a Hebrews 11:6 postscript on our prayers:

Lord, I believe that You are, and that You are a rewarder of those who diligently seek You.

Thank You, God, for gently pursuing our trust.
For reaching for the shattered parts to make us whole.
I trust You with the darkest parts of my past. I know
that Your love for me was as alive and active then as it is now.
You are my Comfort, my Healer, my Restorer.

EXCEPTIONAL FAITH

A Canaanite woman from that region came out and began to cry out, saying, "Have mercy on me, Lord, Son of David; my daughter is cruelly demon-possessed." But He did not answer her a word. And His disciples came and implored Him, saying, "Send her away, because she keeps shouting at us." But He answered and said, "I was sent only to the lost sheep of the house of Israel." But she came and began to bow down before Him, saying, "Lord, help me!"

MATTHEW 15:22–25 NASB

At first glance, it seems like Jesus is unwilling to help a desperate woman. She begged help not for herself, but for her daughter who was being tortured by a demon.

Jesus ignored her. His disciples didn't send her away themselves, or if they tried, good mother that she was, she didn't listen. Having witnessed Jesus interact with all kinds of people, they may have expected Him to respond. Annoyed by her persistence and volume, they finally asked Jesus to get rid of her. But that was never Jesus's intent.

"I was sent only to the lost sheep of the house of Israel," He finally spoke. She was outside the fold. Many are lost, He seemed to be saying, but His focus was Israel's lost. Was He speaking to her or to His disciples? Did that matter or deter this desperate mother? She actually takes that as a green light, approaching Jesus and falling down in front of Him to continue to beg for help.

Jesus's next response would have turned away anyone with an ounce of pride. "It is not good to take the children's bread and throw it to the dogs." Seems harsh, right? But there Jesus had an intent, as He was never without.

She responds, continuing His analogy in wisdom and humility: "Yes," she agrees. "But even the dogs feed on the crumbs which fall from their master's table."

With that, Jesus turns His full attention on her with praise. "O woman, your faith is great; It shall be done for you as you wish."

Jesus stepped out of the blueprint of His ministry, established long before He arrived on earth, to reward the faith of one individual who wouldn't give up.

Jesus is a relationship God, pleased with our belief in Him, our trust in Him. He is not a castor-oil, you'll-thank-me-later god, but a hairs-numbered, your-Father-has-chosen-gladly-to-give-you-the-kingdom God. He's all that. Don't give up.

Jesus, thank You that You are a God who sees individuals and makes exceptions. Thank You for lifting this Samaritan mother's faith up out of history for our example. Give us her persistence, and increase our faith!

THE BODY

He is also head of the body, the church.

COLOSSIANS 1:18 NASB

When I was sixteen, I went on a missions trip to New York. Our team members came from several different states and Canada to train in Missouri before heading to the inner city. It was the farthest I'd ever been from home.

One Sunday we attended a church that met in a large, old theater. The worship was much more . . . full-bodied than I'd ever experienced. My family had attended a few different churches after my parents were saved, and I knew worship to be about facing forward and following along.

Not here. Everyone was their own worship leader. I liked it. Then they called us to the platform.

I think it was spontaneous. I don't remember practicing. But we walked down front, climbed on stage, and stood in a line facing the congregation. We sang a cappella "Sing Alleluia to the Lord." Are you familiar with that one? It's sung in a round, a pretty song, but with a beat that would earn it a spot on Bedtime Classics. Very different from what had been sung.

As our sweet round floated out into the open space, the audience was still. Some glanced at each other and smiled. If I wasn't standing with my team, I would have . . . I don't know, but it was really close to those nightmares where you somehow get to school before realizing you aren't wearing clothes. I looked over my shoulder at a friend, a girl onstage who was part of the worship team. She smiled and winked at me. What a gift. I relaxed a little. After we were done, the band started up with their own rendition of our song, and everyone joined in. It was great.

I love the variety of ways we can praise God. I think He delights in that in individuals too.

Church isn't always a place where variety thrives. I spent a lot of time as an adult going to church just because it was the thing to do. One Sunday, so aware of past experiences and what I didn't like about church, I prayed a simple but honest prayer as I sat there. *Why, Lord? Why church?* And I felt a loving, gentle answer inside: *Because it's Mine.*

The church, even with all its flaws, is still primarily a group of people who belong to Jesus. Scripture calls us His body. And I am part of that. It would be easy to skip if the church were just the dictionary definition I found online: the hierarchy of clergy of a Christian organization. But it is not.

It's Jesus. It's His body: hands, feet, head, heart. Different, but all part of one body. And I want to not only stand and *be* the variety, but be *surrounded* by it as we're held together by our common connection: the Lamb of God who took away the sin of our world.

Jesus, thank You for Your love for us, Your body.
Thank You for giving us the grace to try again.

AT ALL TIMES

God is able to bless you abundantly,
so that in all things at all times, having all that you need,
you will abound in every good work.

2 CORINTHIANS 9:8 NIV

Revelation has normally been the last book that I've turned to in the Bible. It has less to do with its placement than about me being someone anxiety seeks for a BFF. But although the book shows a season when evil will prevail, it also shows us that God knows full well how history will play out, and He will have complete victory in the end. For those whose hearts are His, victory will be in the midst.

Corrie ten Boom and her sister experienced God's

faithfulness during end-times-like evil in a World War II concentration camp. She then traveled around the world proclaiming what her sister said before she died there: *There is no pit so deep that God's love is not deeper.* At a church in Munich, her message was tested when a man approached her.

> One moment I saw the overcoat and the brown hat; the next, a blue uniform and a visored cap with its skull and crossbones. It came back with a rush: the huge room with its harsh overhead lights; the pathetic pile of dresses and shoes in the center of the floor; the shame of walking naked past this man. I could see my sister's frail form ahead of me, ribs sharp beneath the parchment skin.

> As he extended his hand to her, he said "A fine message, *Fräulein*! How good it is to know that, as you say, all our sins are at the bottom of the sea!" He mentioned that he had been a former guard at Ravensbruck. As one prisoner in thousands, she knew he didn't remember her. He had become a Christian, he said. God had forgiven him for his cruelty, he knew. Could his forgiveness come from her as well?

> Would I have been able to forgive someone who had contributed to the drawn-out death of my sister and other members of my family? No.

Neither could she. After what "seemed hours," she sent an arrow prayer to God for help, then stuck her lifeless hand out to the guard's. The story would have been a victory, although hollow, if this were the end. Far from it!

What she describes as a current started in her shoulder, went down her arm, and into their joined hands.

> "'I forgive you, brother!' I cried. 'With all my heart!' For a long moment we grasped each other's hands. . . . I had never known God's love so intensely, as I did then."

God's faithfulness surrounds us before, during, and after difficult times. Corrie later wrote, "Every experience God gives us, every person He puts in our lives is the perfect preparation for the future that only He can see."

That is looking-back wisdom that we can believe as we look forward. God is faithful, He is right there preparing us even in our anxiety and inabilities and in every experience. He can be trusted.

Jesus, thank You for Your victorious ending,
and the gift of You through the lives of others.

DIVINE DETAILS

Lift up your eyes and look to the heavens: Who created all these? He who brings out the starry host one by one and calls forth each of them by name. Because of his great power and mighty strength, not one of them is missing.

ISAIAH 40:26 NIV

God didn't just put the stars in place and call it done. He actively calls to them by name. Is this within the scope of anyone's understanding? There are an estimated billion trillion out there that He protects, making sure none of them go missing. He shepherds the stars.

God's delight with His creation is clearly seen in His intimate concern with the details.

Consider snowflakes. He could have made them all the same, or put them in a few families of similarity, and who would have known it could be any different? Instead, an estimated 15 million billion fall each year, all different.

God delights in variety. If He didn't take shortcuts in creating all the details, even the parts that come in trillions, how much more does He plan and delight in the details that go into the ones created in His image?

When the Lord first called Jeremiah, He indicated that He knew him pre-womb. "Before I formed you in the womb, I knew you" (Jeremiah 1:5). This "knew" isn't just an acknowledgement of our existence. We are pre-known, pre-planned, protected in the identity and place He has for us. Not just pinballs, bouncing off whatever dysfunction pops up in our lives to arrive at who we are when we roll to a stop.

David wrote about God's intimate knowledge of him in Psalm 139. Was this one of the reasons David was called by God a "man after my own heart," because he delighted in the details of their relationship too? David listed the specifics that God knew about him: not just his GPS coordinates, but whether he was sitting or standing; his thoughts; his words before he said them; that God's hand was on him; that there was no place over, under, or around creation, day or night, that would move him out of range of God's love and leading. David acknowledged that God's hand created every part of him; that His thoughts about him outnumbered the grains of sand.

David's words in Psalm 139 are thousands of years old, but still "alive" in their worship of an infinite God, powerful and active, who delights in the details of each one of us. We have not escaped His notice. Just as Jeremiah and David were known, so are you. Known and delighted in.

Father, we could not have imagined a love greater than Yours. Forgive us for thinking You are not interested in everything about us, in the nitty-gritty of our every day.

THE TEACHER

Whatever the Father does,
these things the Son also does in like manner.

JOHN 5:19 NASB

When I was in college, I had to write a paper on Jesus's role as a teacher. His interactions varied so much, but they all had one thing in common. No matter who the individual or how big the crowd or what the subject, He was always asking questions.

Jesus's classroom had no doors. He participated in the public debate that His culture provided, and He lectured on hillsides to thousands. I'm sure He also realized that His every move was teaching, as He put His arms around children, when He overturned tables at the temple, while He was making mud from His own spit to cover a man's eyes. But when the Creator of the universe looked into human eyes, His interactions showed His desire to connect with individuals.

Jesus could have issued statements: It profits a man nothing to gain the whole world if he loses his soul. But a question is interactive. It asks for a response, even if the answer isn't required. What does it profit a man to gain the world and lose his own soul? Rhetorical questions walk away with us. And they are easier to remember.

Jesus was a teaching genius. But when I wrote the paper, I didn't see that He was following in His Father's footsteps.

When Adam and Eve ate from the wrong tree in the garden, God's first course of action was a question: "Where are you?" (Genesis 3:9 NASB). What does it tell us about God when we see Him addressing the distance between them and wanting to hear what happened rather than going right to the consequences?

"I heard the sound of You in the garden, and I was afraid . . . ," Adam responded (verse 10). He recognized the sound of God in the garden because he had heard it before. God walked alongside the ones created in His image. That was the original design and His desired intimacy.

Throughout Scripture, we see God asking questions

and provoking responses that bring His followers into a more intimate relationship with Him. God sent His son to interact with His creation face-to-face, not as a religious leader who taught from the front of a room to others who would also teach and spread the truth. But to connect with everyday people, those who needed Him the most, so the truth of His love would be experienced.

That intimacy is what makes it possible for me to draw strength every day, to experience love, to face my insecurities and fears. I know He is still asking questions and drawing us in to learn how far, how deep, how wide, how awesome His love is for each of us.

Jesus, thank You for coming to us, for being
so approachable and rubbing shoulders with people
that no one else would touch. Thank You for Your love
that continues to come out in questions that show
how intimately You know us and desire to interact with us.
Teach us to love like You.

ONE MORE

*For the Son of Man has come to seek
and to save that which was lost.*

LUKE 19:10 NASB

Desmond Doss enlisted in the army after Pearl Harbor. He went into combat as a medic, refusing to carry a weapon because of his convictions that killing was wrong. His story is told in the movie I saw recently, *Hacksaw Ridge*.

When his unit ascended a cliff 350 feet high on Okinawa Island, the enemy attacked with mortar and machine gun fire at the top, leaving many dead or wounded. Doss remained after most of his unit withdrew, searching out the wounded to within just a few yards from the enemy. He then carried them to the edge of the cliff, where he faced a dilemma.

"I didn't have enough rope to do the job like it should be done, then the Lord brought to my mind [a] knot I learned in West Virginia that I'd never seen or heard of before." . . . Doss fashioned a special sling that enabled him to lower the men one by one to safety. "So I just kept prayin', 'Lord, please help me get more and more, one more, until there was none left, and I'm the last one down'" (*Medal of Honor: Oral Histories*).

He estimates that he saved about fifty. Others in his unit said one hundred. The official record on his Medal of Honor was seventy-five. He faced almost certain death as he carried them one by one to the edge, without knowing beforehand how he was going to get that first one down! He valued the life of his friends over his own, sharing the convictions of his God, who places high value on each individual.

There are hundreds—likely thousands—of people here today, children, grandchildren, and great-grandchildren, of the men that Desmond Doss rescued.

"I know who I owe my life to, as well as my men," he said. "That's why I like to tell this story to the glory of God, because I know from the human standpoint, I should not be here" (*Medal of Honor: Oral Histories*).

As I sat in the movie theater, watching the actor who played Desmond continue to go back for one more, tears came to my eyes as Luke 19:10 played in my mind, "The Son of Man has come to seek and to save that which was lost." We were guaranteed dead without His sacrificial love.

I'm so glad Desmond Doss's story was not buried under the years that came after. We need to hear about this man who stood in his conviction, took abuse for his apparent "weakness" from the very men whose lives he would save. This conviction came, in part, from witnessing violence when he was growing up. His imperfect past contributed to the man he became, whom God chose to display great courage and protection and show Himself to the world. We can be sure that He does that for us too. He does not leave one of us behind, but redeems and turns us into trophies of His strength.

Jesus, thank You for the reflection of You in Desmond Doss. Help us to trust Your faithfulness even when we don't see the next step, and to love like You do, sacrificially.

OUR PROVIDER

*The LORD God made garments of skin
for Adam and his wife, and clothed them.*

GENESIS 3:21 NASB

"Go get dressed," God could have told Adam and Eve after they sinned and were aware of their nakedness. But God moved close, and not only provided covering, but clothed them. Sin did not stop Him from being their Provider. From everything we see in Scripture, He wants us to be confident of that.

When the Israelites were in the wilderness, God provided manna, this strange but wonderful ready-to-eat food in a culture where preparing a meal usually involved slaughtering an animal. This stuff appears on the ground, ready for consumption. Like Twinkies. (But likely good for you.) In instructing them to collect enough for only one day, God was trying to train them to trust Him. Day after day after day, they had what they needed; God could be trusted. The day after they ate the produce of the promised land, the manna was no longer there in the morning (Joshua 5:12).

Once they entered the promised land, God laid out a strategy for the Israelites that would bring down the walls of Jericho. He told the Israelites to take no plunder from the city. Only the silver and gold and bronze and iron were to be collected for the treasury of the Lord. When the Lord flattened the walls before them, one Israelite did not follow the Lord's instruction, and it affected the whole nation. God did not say "good enough." He expected the trust and faithfulness of every individual.

I doubt if the riches of Jericho would have been tempting for me, given God's track record of provision in the wilderness and His unmistakable instructions. But do I trust Him with my needs and the needs of my family today? Do I have enough trust in Him today to walk away from a sure thing, or would I just open wide my arms and sweep as much into my lap as I could?

Jesus promises provision when we prioritize Him. These instructions are beautifully unmistakable also:

Do not worry then, saying, "What will we eat?" or "What will we drink?" or "What will we wear for clothing?" For the Gentiles eagerly seek all these things; for your heavenly Father knows that you need all these things. But seek first His kingdom and His righteousness, and all these things will be added to you (Matthew 6:31–33).

He doesn't want us see Him out of the corner of our eye while our needs take full screen. He will give us confidence, an eyes-on-Him confidence, that He will do what He says He will do: provide when we prioritize Him first in our lives.

I will trust in my Provider. I will purpose to believe every day what His Word says: that He rewards those who diligently seek Him. And where I have questions about how things have turned out in the past, I will remember His faithfulness in the middle of it, and trust Him with the questions unanswered.

Thank You, Father, for Your trustworthiness,
for Your love that carries us through the questions.

LIES WE BELIEVE

The thief comes only to steal and kill and destroy;
I have come that they may have life, and have it to the full.

JOHN 10:10 NIV

I texted my sister, panicked about meeting a deadline, and she came back with something I'd never heard before: The lies that we believe about ourselves shout the loudest when we are under stress.

So true. These accusations can lay dormant for a while, but roar to life in the stress of trying to counter them. Sometimes they attach to things we heard growing up or things we've latched onto in ourselves.

- You can't accomplish anything.
- You're just not smart.
- You're a homely little thing.
- No one really likes you.
- You just don't have what it takes.

The Bible calls Satan the accuser. And says that he comes to kill, steal, and destroy. His targets include our hope, self-esteem, and faith in a powerful, loving God. And we better believe he knows what he can get us to fall for, with his intent to cripple.

When my first pregnancy ended in miscarriage, I thought: *Of course my body failed at sustaining the life of our baby, something a woman's body is designed to do. I am a failure as a female.*

I had always felt like the boy growing up in our family of girls. I looked a lot more like my father than my mother. My large hands were a constant reminder of his. ("Stand Up and Greet Somebody" time in church was brutal.) I always felt outside the female fold. Back then I didn't see the power of that on my unfolding identity.

I didn't address it then, either. But the time came when I could look it straight in the eye and pray about it. My sister prayed too. And I confessed out loud my belief in being fearfully and wonderfully made, unique in my femininity. It's hard for me to even write that word. I know the issue is not totally gone, but I noticed a difference immediately.

The lies Satan whispers into our ears are just that—lies. God has the power and the desire to correct distortions in our self-perception, to overcome the lies, to get us back on track to what He has called us to be. Each of us is fearfully and wonderfully made.

Lord, expose what we believe about ourselves
that does not line up with Your thoughts about us.
Let our confessions be Your truth as we move
into the plan of freedom and wholeness You have for us.

FORGIVENESS

*Do you think lightly of the riches of His kindness
and tolerance and patience,
not knowing that the kindness of God
leads you to repentance?*

ROMANS 2:4 NASB

When I worked at a rehab center in Chicago as a college student, we had a client who was vocal in her stand against abortion. She was a prostitute. She had eight kids.

Over twenty years later, I stood in the med room of the facility where I worked, facing a young woman who had just had an abortion. I had been asked to drive her to this appointment. The staff understood when I declined. I wasn't the only one to decline. But a driver had been found.

She asked about the fullness in her breasts. Her milk had started to come in. She seemed almost upbeat when she asked if I knew how long that would last. Tears involuntarily filled my eyes. Her body was still trying to provide for that little one, even though he or she was gone.

That young girl wasn't the first to check into treatment wanting an abortion. When I encountered the first one, I had approached and asked if she was willing to keep the baby. I knew a couple who had been on an adoption waiting list. Later she told me she had asked the father about the possibility, and he had said, "Absolutely not." Abortion was the only option. I prayed about it. Later I got the sad news that she miscarried.

But the woman I was asked to drive and others went through with their abortions. I hadn't approached them beforehand. I don't have a good answer for why not. No matter what circumstances each of those children would have been born with or into, each had unique qualities, gifts, and talents that the world will never know. Gianna Jessen, who survived a saline abortion when her mother was thirty weeks pregnant, has grown up with cerebral palsy as a result, said: "I'm invading the culture as an unconventional woman, just being me. The beautiful thing about having cerebral palsy is it's part of my sermon . . . God has a way of making the most miserable thing beautiful."

Recently I heard a priest on the radio relaying a conversation he'd had years ago in which he'd tried to talk a young woman out of an abortion, but couldn't. His parting remark was that he would love her either way, but he wished she would reconsider. Years later, someone came up to him and introduced herself as the child that woman did not abort. His "I'll love you either way" comment was what made the difference, he found out.

Just as the priest's kindness changed this young woman's mind, God's kindness changes us. When we ask for it, His forgiveness covers life-taking decisions, as well as unspoken suggestions.

Jesus, thank You for the great value we have in Your eyes.
Give us fervency in our desire to reach out to others
with the kindness You've shown us.

DO-OVER

And the God of all grace, who called you
to his eternal glory in Christ ... will himself restore you
and make you strong, firm and steadfast.

1 PETER 5:10 NIV

Years ago my sister told me that she wished she could have
a do-over with her kids. At the time, I thought that was
terrible thing to say about them. I liked her kids. I didn't
say anything to her, but she would likely have corrected
me if I had. It wasn't until years later, when I had kids of
my own, that I realized I had misunderstood: Her comment was directed at herself, not at them.

Regrets can come into focus quickly with our children.

I wish I would have had more grace with my oldest, given more attention to my middle, been more consistent with my youngest. I wish I would have given them things more often just because they're mine, and less as rewards earned for good behavior. I wish I would have followed the lead of the heavenly Father. At two significant events in Jesus's life, His Father couldn't hold back, and proud words spilled from heaven: "This is my beloved son, in whom I'm well pleased. . . ." His words claimed Jesus, loved Jesus, and affirmed His pleasure in Him.

I've noticed that when I look for ways to build my boys up, to show little pleasures, it changes the atmosphere in our house. Little things, like:

- How my oldest poured two glasses of lemonade and did not keep the bigger glass for himself
- How my youngest made eye contact with a store clerk and said thank you
- How my middle one was dressed—putting plaid shorts and a striped t-shirt together that looked really good

It can be easy to let the regrets take control. We have an enemy who has a strategy to bring us down. But we also have a God who loves us with generous affirmation, who is quick to forgive and is generous in all of our do-overs in our journey to become like Him. And when a do-over is not possible, He offers us forgiveness and restoration while giving us wisdom to love in the current season of life.

Father, thank You for the example of Your words
that came from heaven and covered Jesus with Your favor.
Give us eyes to see the things, no matter how big or small,
that can to be called out to affirm those we love today.

WHAT ABOUT YOU?

*He said to them, "But who do you say that I am?" Simon
Peter answered, "You are the Christ, the Son of the
living God." And Jesus said to him, "Blessed are
you, Simon Barjona, because flesh and blood did not
reveal this to you, but My Father who is in heaven.
I also say to you that you are Peter,
and upon this rock I will build My church."*

MATTHEW 16:15–18 NASB

When Jesus asked His disciples what people were saying
about His identity, they gave Him a good cross section
sample: John the Baptist, Elijah, Jeremiah. The disciples
were well aware that people thought He was someone

great, even supernatural. Jesus must have known it too. With the opinion of others' still fresh in their minds, He turned the question on them: What about you?

Jesus knew what others were saying. He wanted to know how those closest to Him would choose to answer. I wonder if there was a pause, or if Peter jumped in right away identifying Him as the Christ, Son of the living God.

Jesus responded by calling Peter blessed with a revelation he did not pull from those around him, or even from himself. Once Peter, known as Simon, identified Jesus, Jesus identified him with a new name: Peter, meaning rock.

Names mean something to God. When God gave Abraham and Sarah their new names, it was an eternal reminder of the long-held purpose that He had for them. Psalm 147:4 tells us God numbers the stars and calls them all by name. Tucked in the second chapter of Revelation, we read about God giving those who overcome, a white stone on which is written a new name that no one knows but he who receives it (Revelation 2:17).

Jesus said, "You are Peter, and upon this rock I will build My church." There are differing opinions about what Jesus meant by "this." I believe Jesus was referring to Peter's answer. The truth of the revelation that God Himself speaks into individual hearts, like He did Peter's: Jesus is the Son of the living God.

After Peter denied Jesus, I bet Satan the accuser was

right in his ear: *And you said that you would die for him. What a joke! You are so weak, He knew you'd deny Him.* Then, maybe someone called him by his God-given name. Rock. A word Samuel, Moses, and David had all used to describe God in Scripture. Jesus identified him as Peter, strength.

Jesus asks that question today to us: Who do you say that I am? Our answer to His identity will determine our own. Will we reach out and take hold of the person He has planned for us to become?

Who will you say that He is?

Jesus, You are the Christ, the Son of the living God. Thank You for Your interest in the specifics of naming throughout Scripture. Thank You for the new identity You give us, regardless of what we feel.

SISTERS

She went back and called her sister Mary aside.
"The Teacher is here," she said, "and is asking for you."

JOHN 11:28 NIV

The Gospel of Luke gives us a very real picture of the difficulty between sisters and the way Jesus loved them as individuals.

Martha welcomed Jesus and His disciples into her home as they were "on their way," and starts preparations, apparently for a meal. An impressive act of spontaneous hospitality for such a large group. But while she worked, her sister Mary stayed at the feet of Jesus.

Of course, this irked Martha. Jesus was so approachable,

Martha tried to enlist Him to light a fire under her sister. I wonder if she talked to Jesus in front of everyone, with Mary right there.

"Lord, don't You care that my sister has left me to do the work by myself? Tell her to help me!" (Luke 10:40 NIV).

Siblings have an inborn ability to know when they are doing more work than their sister or brother. (Even when they aren't, said the mom.) But instead of attempting to redistribute the workload, Jesus gently redirects Martha. "Martha, Martha, you are worried and upset about many things." He lets her know He sees her anxiety before telling her that He wasn't going to send Mary away from Him. "Few things are needed—or indeed only one. Mary has chosen what is better, and it will not be taken away from her" (Luke 10:41–42 NIV).

God creates such diversity between people who share the same gene pool. Martha had a love that presented itself in service. She was a confident host, welcoming the large group in. Mary was wired to express her love more emotionally.

When their brother Lazarus was sick, the sisters sent word to Jesus. "Lord, the one you love is sick" (John 11:3). When Jesus arrived, Martha met Him on the road. They spoke about life, death, and resurrection, and He ended with a question for her. "Everyone who lives and believes in me will never die. Do you believe this?" She did.

She came back hopeful and whispered to her sister, "The teacher is here and is asking for you." Mary quickly left, and when she reached Jesus, she fell down at His feet. There is little conversation. Mary is crying. Surrounded by sorrow, Jesus also cries. Even with His resurrection of Lazarus just minutes away.

Jesus accepted how each sister showed their love for Him. It was authentically them.

We all love, share, work in our own unique way. The ways of our siblings or friends can drive us crazy or drive us to envy. But we are created to be different and to embrace and reflect Gods' love in a distinct, individualized way. God loves to see the diversity.

Jesus, thank You for how You love and comfort my sisters,
thank You for how You embrace us so differently.
Let my words be like Martha's,
whispering of Your calling to them.

STARTING OVER

The LORD's lovingkindnesses . . . are new every morning.
LAMENTATIONS 3:22–23 NASB

Some mornings, life seems so much more difficult than others. My sister told me of her experience with a little guy who was having a terrible day at the school where she taught kindergarten, and how he suddenly was changed.

Johnny yelled and slapped at his dad who was trying to get him into the classroom. Other parents and students moved to get out of the way, the final mom mouthing to my sister "I'll pray for you" as the mom left. My sister let go of Johnny's hand to get the classroom door closed, then started toward the carpet where the children had gathered for their morning activities. Johnny had fled to the corner, and when he ignored my sister's request to join them, she started toward him. His response was classic.

He shouted, "You're not going to win this one, Mrs. Vallin!" She said his little foot began to strike the ground as he backed up like a bull ready to charge. "And charge he did! I could hear gasps coming from the other children as he took off across the room toward me."

By the look on his face, he was shocked he hadn't bowled her over. He went back to the beanbag chair in the corner, and my sister silently prayed for him as she went through the morning exercises. She stopped once to invite him to join them. He answered with a screech.

The next thing she knew, Johnny was standing erect beside his beanbag chair, reciting the books of the Bible with the others. After the memory work, she again asked him if he was ready to join the class and he said, "Yes, Mrs. Vallin."

A few hours later the children were preparing for snack when Johnny sat next to her. They began visiting and Johnny told her how nice Jesus is and how good it feels when He touches you. She agreed with him and asked if he'd felt Jesus touch him. He said, "Yes, when I was sitting in the beanbag I was mad at you but then Jesus came and stood by me. He put His hand on top of my head." She asked if Jesus said anything to him and John responded,

"He told me to be kind and obey." He then hugged her before he skipped off to play.

Isn't that great? When I've had my own version of pawing the ground and charging, the same thing brings me back around: an encounter with His love. Once, after struggling for hours, I finally asked God for a verse, and Isaiah 40:11 popped into my mind. I looked it up and found His words for me: "Like a shepherd He will tend His flock; in His arms He will gather the lambs and carry them in His bosom; He will gently lead the nursing ewes." It was exactly what I needed.

He comes to us differently, just for the asking. We can start our day over with Him.

Jesus, thank You for Your lovingkindness that leads us
to repentance and a day transformed.

FREE THINKER

I am the vine, you are the branches;
he who abides in Me and I in him, he bears much fruit,
for apart from Me you can do nothing.

JOHN 15:5 NASB

I've always had a love/hate relationship with outlines. They have their place, in a class syllabus and other steps to understanding. I love the idea of the structure they offer, but only on paper.

For years, I've tried hard to detail what my schedule will look like. When I don't follow it, I feel like a failure for a while, then eventually rewrite it and try again. I have decades of notebooks with random pages that give testimony to my effort to stay on a daily routine, diet regiment, prayer schedule. Yet I remember as a kid feeling taxed by having to brush my teeth every single night.

In my twenties, when someone asked what I wanted to do with my life, I said I wanted to be a free thinker. It was partly a joke, to throw off from an answer I wasn't confident enough yet to say. (I wanted to do something creative, maybe become a writer.) The desire was always there to live outside the lines. The how-to realization for that came later: Even free thinkers need self-discipline and consistency. Two areas that have never been my strength.

I tell myself it's because I scored highest in the creative quadrant of a test I took in high school that measures your *bent*. But I've come to see the beautiful reality that God uses people like me, despite such consistent inconsistency and underpinnings of personal chaos. I smile at that. Because there I am.

My life will always wax and wane, maybe even more than the average Jill. My days are inconsistent, so are my emotions and self-acceptance. But here is truth: God. He defies outlines and logic and loves me beyond my understanding.

A friend of mine who was in and out of prison several times said, "When I finally figured out that I can't figure it out, things started to turn around for me. I realized that there are no plans of my own that can help. It is always and only about Jesus."

As much as I want to check that huge "Amen" off my things-learned list, it needs to be realized every day. It is, I believe, what *abiding* means. Continually looking to the One who knows us more intimately than we know ourselves.

God is a God of order, not confusion or chaos (1 Corinthians 14:33), but He gives us priorities and meetings in our day that aren't meant to follow a Roman numeral. Oswald Chambers wrote, "Live in a constant state of expectancy, and leave room for God to come in as He decides." His plans are beyond the ability of this free thinker to imagine.

Jesus, thank You for the peace and order that You bring,
and Your desire for us to lean on You,
not our own understanding.

THE LIGHT OF LIFE

I am the Light of the world; he who follows Me
will not walk in the darkness,
but will have the Light of life.

JOHN 8:12 NASB

In the last verse of his Gospel, John signs off by saying that the whole world wouldn't be able to contain the books if all the details of Jesus's life were to be written. How did John decide what to include? Knowing the importance, it would seem to be the perfect storm for writer's block. Except that Jesus was a very present reality long after John could no longer physically lean against Him during a meal. Jesus said He would be with them always. He would bring things back to their remembrance. He would send a Helper.

John started his account with Jesus's time-transcending existence: "In the beginning the Word already existed. . . . The Word gave life to everything that was created, and his life brought light to everyone" (John 1:1–4 NLT).

John uses the word *light* five times in the first few verses to introduce Jesus. "I am the light of the world," John quotes Jesus in chapter 8, immediately after the incident of the woman caught in adultery. It was a story about sin—the woman's, and those holding the stones. Jesus told the ones holding the stones to go ahead and stone her, if they had no sin of their own. The woman whose sin was brought to the Light walked away forgiven. The stone-holders just walked away, their sin not exposed or forgiven.

We have the promise from the Light Himself: When we follow Him, we don't walk in darkness. I'm learning that it's a belly-up-to-the-Light-and-refuse-to-walk-away approach when I see my inability or failure spotlighted. But all I want to do is exit.

I did that one time. Slammed out of the house and ended up at a park, where I had the God-implanted sense to face Him full-on about it. I took a paper and pencil in hand and pushed in asking and started to write. Words that may have seemed like common sense to others were a revelation to me for the situation.

When we've turned ourselves inside out to Him, even pushed out the corners to show there is nothing we are holding back or hiding behind, and invite Him into the middle of it, something happens. It may not always be immediate, but we can trust in His faithfulness.

He will guide us in the life He's called us to, and the purpose He wants to fulfill in us. The same Helper who guided John as he wrote, also desires to give us inspiration for resolving what we face day by day.

We won't walk in darkness for long.

Jesus, thank You for being our timeless Helper
and Light of Life.

OUTERWEAR

Man looks at the outward appearance,
but the LORD looks at the heart.

1 SAMUEL 16:7 NASB

My pastor once said that he hears a lot of comments about how he dresses. He wears dress shirts that don't need to be tucked in. (The traditional service attenders may not agree with that.)

When I was in high school, our pastor wore three piece suits exclusively. He rarely took his suit coat off, and when he did, it seemed to make him uncomfortable. One of the teachers of my small church-school commented that her pastor back home preached in polo shirts. Of course, I didn't believe her (tell me more about this strange land . . . this *California*).

At twenty-three, Catherine Marshall found herself the pastor's wife at one of the oldest churches in Washington D.C. It had traditions that reached back to 1803. She was mentored in those traditions, as well as in the expectation of fashion and social protocol in her role as pastor's wife.

It seemed like a perfect setup for shallow, appearance-focused religion. That would have been a faulty conclusion about her.

Yes, Catherine was a formal person. I doubt if anyone called her Cathy. Ever. But she wrote with such maskless, searching honesty and insight, once I finished *Something More*, I searched out her other books. Sometimes they came from one of my sisters. She and I don't share a common interest in many authors, but Catherine Marshall bridges that gap.

I've made that mistake before, let myself get distracted by the external. It's the partiality that James 2 warns about, only in the opposite direction. I feel uncomfortable when large worship teams coordinate what they wear. (Are we trying to put on a variety show?) There was a time when I looked at what people were wearing and the expressions on their faces as they walked down the center aisle to the front pew and concluded that they were not there to worship.

Their hearts are not in the right place. That's what was running through my head years ago as I sat under the balcony one Sunday morning. I remember it because, as the thought came, the Lord spoke to me. In His gentleness, He said: *And where is your heart?* If they were focused on themselves, we had something in common: So was I. (Thank You, Lord.)

Our focus, my focus, has to be on Him. It's not about what someone is or isn't wearing. To tuck or not to tuck. It's about the purity of the heart.

Jesus, thank You for the variety that is in Your body, and for Your direction in what's most important.

ANSWERING THE CALL

The Lord is the one who goes ahead of you;
He will be with you.
He will not fail you or forsake you.
Do not fear or be dismayed.

DEUTERONOMY 31:8 NASB

When Samuel first told Saul about God's calling him to be Israel's first king, Saul questioned his qualifications because of his family background. "Am I not a Benjamite, of the smallest of the tribes of Israel, and my family the least of all the families . . . ?" (1 Samuel 9:21 NASB).

Samuel said, "The Spirit of the Lord will come upon you mightily, and you shall prophecy with them and be changed into another man" (1 Samuel 10:6). Saul had no footsteps to follow, but if the Spirit of the Lord would come and change him, he could have grabbed onto that with both hands.

Saul had never prophesied before, and when it happened, it really got people talking. Yet when he arrived back home, even when asked point-blank, "Please tell me what Samuel said to you" (verse 15), he left out the part about Samuel anointing his head with oil, kissing him, and proclaiming, "Has not the Lord anointed you a ruler over His inheritance?" (verse 1).

It appears Saul wasn't believing His calling.

When Samuel called the Israelites together to reveal their king, he delivered a message from God. "You have today rejected your God, who delivers you from all your calamities and your distresses . . . you have said, 'No, but set a king over us'" (1 Samuel 10:19).

How is that for an inaugural introduction? Samuel told the people to present themselves before the Lord by tribe and by clan until the Lord revealed the new king. Saul knew the spotlight was coming. When the selection process of drawing lots finally pointed to him, the Lord had to disclose his location: "He is hiding himself by the baggage" (verse 22).

It seems to me Saul had been hiding in the baggage since Samuel first anointed him. He was distracted by his own inadequacy. He thought the sum total of his calling was himself.

When they found Saul in the baggage, the Israelites "took him from there" (verse 23). He became king. But almost immediately in his reign, when under pressure, he showed his lack of trust in the One who had called him.

Saul could have been something different. He wasn't chosen to fail: "The LORD would have established your kingdom over Israel forever. But now your kingdom shall not endure. The LORD has sought out for Himself a man after His own heart" (1 Samuel 13:13–14).

The Lord knows that without Him we can do nothing. We step successfully into His outrageous plan for us not by looking back, at who we come from, or by looking down, at ourselves, but by looking to Him. He will bring it to pass. When we make Him Lord of our hearts, He becomes the backbone of our lives, the completer of our dreams.

Lord, give us hearts to seek You, and strength to boldly face
Your calling for us. Don't let us be dismayed or shrink back
from our part in revealing Your glory.

THE WALK

He delights in unchanging love.

MICAH 7:18 NASB

I have fallen to temptation many times by failing to believe that God loves me, is true to His Word, and has my best interest at heart. Eve fell for that, too.

> Serpent: "Indeed, has God said, 'You shall not eat from any tree of the garden?'"
> Eve: "From the fruit of the tree which is in the middle of the garden, God has said, 'You shall not eat from it or touch it, or you will die.'"
> Serpent: "You surely will not die! For God knows

that in the day you eat from it, your eyes will be opened, and you will be like God, knowing good and evil" (Genesis 3:1–4).

Satan was making it look like God was holding out on them. When she first heard Satan's smooth intro, "Indeed, has God said . . ." she should have run to the spot in the garden where God had walked with them and called out, "God, are You here yet? I need You!" She didn't. She listened and pondered and . . . sinned.

When Eve and Adam sinned, they were the ones who stepped away first. Their broken relationship was evident by the distance shame produced. But God stepped forward, looking. "Where are you?"

That original sin succeeded in alienating us from a personal walk with a perfect Creator. But it wasn't the final word.

Jesus, the Word made flesh, brought us back in. He paid the penalty for the sin that separated us from His Father. We get to walk with God again when we accept the forgiveness He paid for.

Hebrews 11:1 defines faith as the assurance of things hoped for. Faith is a belief that despite what my feelings tell me, I can know that He is for me and with me. It counters my temptation at times to believe that God's goodness is castor oil and a distant You'll thank me later.

No. God set up that walk and looks for it even more than I do.

One of God's intentions for the Israelites' long wilderness walk was to teach His people that He is the dependable source of all they receive.

> He led you through the great and terrible wilderness, with its fiery serpents and scorpions and thirsty ground where there was no water . . . that He might test you, to do good for you in the end. Otherwise, you may say in your heart, "My power and the strength of my hand made me this wealth." (Deuteronomy 8:15–17 NASB)

The wilderness walk was a training in trust before incredible blessing.

Whether we are walking in a garden, surrounded by everything we need, or a wilderness, surrounded by nothing, His love for us and intention for good is unchanging.

Jesus, thank You for Your sacrifice for me
that brought us back to the Father.
Help me to trust You more today than I did yesterday.

THE AGED

*Stand up in the presence of the aged, show respect
for the elderly and revere your God. I am the LORD.*

LEVITICUS 19:32 NIV

Sitting in a hospital waiting room, I overheard a conversation between a nurse and a ninety-seven-year-old man in a wheelchair. She complimented him loudly on his age, and he replied by questioning his purpose.

"You keep Dorothy company," the nurse offered cheerfully.

"That's it," he said quietly.

"If the roles were reversed, you would do the same, you would take care of her."

He agreed, but added after a short pause, "I have nothing to do."

I never realized until spending time with my eighty-six-year-old mother-in-law how often the word *old* is used in a derogatory way. Like something used up. That's what Abraham's wife Sarah thought when she overheard the Lord telling Abraham that she would have a baby at ninety. "After I am worn out and my lord is old, will I now have this pleasure?" (Genesis 18:12).

Sarah was feeling the years and saw herself as worn out. I wonder how it went taking care of an infant. I bet it gave her new life.

God values the elderly, as reflected in His direction in Leviticus to stand up in their presence. He connects our respect for them with our reverence for Him. He has shown us over and over that He does not put His people out to pasture.

Noah did not become a father or finish the ark until after he was 500; God waited until Abraham was a childless seventy-five to call him; Daniel was in in his eighties when he spent the night in the lions' den, and later was greeted by an angel with the greeting, "Daniel, you who are highly esteemed . . ." (Daniel 10:11).

Then, of course, there is Moses, who knew of his calling as deliverer of his people and tried to step into it before his time. Acts 7:25 (NASB) says, "And he supposed that his brethren understood that God was granting them deliverance through him, but they did not understand." He spent forty years in a wilderness until God showed up unmistakably and led him at eighty into his calling. There he stayed until he was well over 100.

The man in the wheelchair at the hospital would have been not quite halfway through that gig. Even though this sweet man felt useless, he was not. I wish I would have talked to him about his life and the history he lived through. What a rare gift to be able to hear about the 1920s and 30s from someone who lived them. Wouldn't it be great if he could be sharing his life with a younger generation?

"Remember the days of old; consider the generations long past. Ask your father and he will tell you, your elders, and they will explain to you" (Deuteronomy 32:7 NIV).

Jesus, thank You for Your presence and faithfulness
to the very end of our lives. Thank You also for the blessing
of the elderly. Help us to seek them out with respect,
to include and engage them.

ACCOMPLISH

The LORD will accomplish what concerns me;
Your lovingkindness, O LORD, is everlasting.

PSALM 138:8 NASB

When Saul was publicly crowned as king, there were some men who did not think him capable. "How can this one deliver us?" they asked, and not just to themselves. They despised him . . . but Saul kept silent (1 Samuel 10:27). It was the inadequacy Saul had felt, coming from the mouths of others.

Saul's first recorded battle as king was such a resounding victory over the Ammonites that it says no two survivors were left together. The people wanted to bring out the men who had despised Saul and kill them then and there.

Saul would not allow them to be touched. "Not a man shall be put to death this day, for today the LORD has accomplished deliverance in Israel" (1 Samuel 11:13). Awesome! Don't you just want Saul, the underdog from a tiny tribe, with no credentials to speak of, to be a great king? He started out that way, crediting the victory to God.

Enter the Philistine battle, two chapters later. Fear came on the Israelites as they saw the enemy "like the sand which is on the seashore in abundance." Saul's own men were trembling with fear and those who had assembled to help them started to leave.

Samuel had instructed Saul to wait for seven days for him, then he would make the burnt offering and the peace offering in front of the assembled army. But as Saul saw people leaving, he made a decision that would cost him. He made the offerings himself.

They eventually beat the Philistines—after Saul's son Jonathan went into battle with just his armor-bearer, and the Lord caused the Philistines to turn on themselves. The Israelites who had previously fled came out to help pursue the fleeing army.

God brought back what Saul thought was lost. He won the battle. But in not waiting for Samuel to offer the sacrifices, he had lost the kingdom. Samuel said, "The LORD has sought out for Himself a man after His own heart, and the LORD has appointed him as ruler over His people, because you have not kept what the LORD commanded you" (1 Samuel 13:14 NASB).

In the high prebattle stress, Saul probably had a memory of *"Can this one deliver us?"* playing in his mind as he waited for Samuel. And waited. As soon as he decided to take those sacrifices into his own hands, Samuel showed up.

God was looking for a relationship, one who sought out His heart, and He found him in a fifteen-year-old shepherd boy whom He had already appointed as ruler. Saul's choices took him away from the man and king God had called him to be. The kingdom legacy for his family was not to be.

Are you letting the perceived thoughts or whispers or even body language of others hinder you from believing what God says about you? *You* are not the same person as *You and God.* He sees so much more in us than we do in ourselves. Let's look to Him and walk in the person and plan He has for us.

Father, thank You that we don't have to depend
on ourselves for the strength of our callings.
Give us strength to, day after day after day,
lean on You and not our own understanding.

DO YOU SEE THIS WOMAN?

As she stood behind him at his feet weeping,
she began to wet his feet with her tears.

LUKE 7:38 NIV

A woman with a reputation as a sinner had heard that Jesus was having dinner at the house of a Pharisee, so she took a vial of perfume and headed over uninvited.

I don't picture her knocking. It didn't seem that she was concerned about what the other guests thought as she went to Jesus's feet.

He sat there as she kissed His feet continually and didn't ask her to stop. He didn't move as she wept and her tears fell, and her hair—something prized and usually covered—caressed His feet. He watched as she poured out the perfume, unwilling to interrupt her sacrificial display of love.

The thoughts of the Pharisee were clear to Him: *If this man were a prophet He would know who and what sort of person this woman is who is touching Him* (Luke 7:39 NASB).

Turning to the host, he said, "Simon, I have something to say to you" (verse 40). At Simon's welcome, He tells a story about two debtors being forgiven; one a little, one a lot. Then He turned toward the woman.

> Do you see this woman? I entered your house; you gave Me no water for My feet, but she has wet My feet with her tears and wiped them with her hair. You gave Me no kiss; but she, since the time I came in, has not ceased to kiss My feet. You did not anoint My head with oil, but she anointed My feet with perfume. For this reason I say to you, her sins, which are many, have been forgiven, for she loved much; but he who is forgiven little, loves little. (Luke 7:44–47)

Simon's identity as a Pharisee rested on his separateness, as one who held strictly to the law. The meaning of the word *Pharisee* reveals that identity: *one who is separate*. Yet this woman was better able to keep the commandment revealed by Jesus as the greatest: to love God with your heart, soul, mind, and strength.

When Jesus spoke to her directly, He addressed His love for her in, "Your sins are forgiven. . . . Your faith has saved you" (verse 50). Then, finally, He sends her away in peace.

This sinful woman's cup was flowing over with the love God had for her. It spilled out of her eyes and into her caresses and kisses on the feet of her Savior. His acceptance and forgiveness had so washed away her shame that she had no concern whatever what those around her thought.

When I was in grade school, my Sunday school teacher invited anyone to stay in the room after class who wanted to pray to accept Jesus. I wanted to stay, but was intimidated by what others would think of me. I stayed only because my friend Cora did. I didn't like that about myself.

But Jesus is so welcoming and accepting. The more I focus on Him, the easier it is to love others and let their opinions go. God wants to fill our hearts with His fullness, like He did for the woman in this story, and send us away in peace.

Jesus, let our worship be a reflection
of what we see in Your eyes.

KNOWN

"'You shall love the L<small>ORD</small> your God with all your heart,
and with all your soul, and with all your mind.
This is the great and foremost commandment.
The second is like it, 'You shall love your neighbor as
yourself.' On these two commandments depend
the whole Law and the Prophets."

MATTHEW 22:37–40 <small>NASB</small>

Does anybody else find it beyond the scope of their brain that the Creator of the Universe, the Host of Heaven's armies, has so much more than just a passing affection for us?

In Psalm 139, David said that God is the One who not

only laid out plans of us, but physically "knit" us together in the womb. The psalm reads like a love letter to God, acknowledging God's intimate knowledge of his thoughts, his words, even his body position. And David's prayer at the end is a natural result; he invites God to search him and get rid of anything in him that shouldn't be there. When we come face-to-face with the reality of God's intense love for us, it opens our arms and our fists. We become willing to let things go.

When Jesus was asked about the greatest commandment, He could have said, "They are all equally important. Do not let one escape at the expense of another." He didn't. He responded immediately, "Love the Lord your God with all your heart, with all your soul, and with all your mind." In asking for our love, He is asking us to know Him intimately, as David did. To know His voice, His whispering words that help us and heal us and bring us to a place we cannot reach on our own.

Jesus saw fit to mention a second commandment—to love our neighbors as ourselves. "On these two depend all the law and the prophets," He said. Their law—Genesis, Exodus, Leviticus, Numbers, and Deuteronomy—depend on our all-encompassing love for God and each other. That wonderfully confusing statement from Jesus makes me smile. The details in those books, much of which I find hard to read (Leviticus, I'm talking to you), are about God's love for us.

These five books were the Word of God that David loved so much. He read about God calling Abraham out, changing his name, calling him friend.

God's love calls each of us out, away from what we've always known, to be known by Him—like He was known to Abraham. He is searching our hearts to see if we are ready to love and know Him intimately.

Jesus, thank You for templating everything on love. Show us how it looks to love You with each of the parts You specified. My heart, I can understand, but my soul, and my might? Thank You for a love so great it goes beyond me. Let Your love come down powerfully on the one reading this now who may need help understanding and feeling You.

PATHS

I will give them one heart [a new heart],
and put a new spirit within them. I will take from them
the heart of stone, and will give them a heart of flesh
[that is responsive to My touch].

EZEKIEL 11:19 AMP

When I was in Bible school in Chicago, part of my practical work included helping the chaplain at a large juvenile detention center get ready for church services. Sometimes the chaplain preached, but most of the time other churches came in and gave the message. One Sunday, the chaplain told us that *we* would be doing an upcoming service. The two guys that I volunteered with would give the message to the boys, and I would speak to the girls.

You should know that this was continents out of my comfort zone.

Other churches had speakers come in who gave testimonies of God's redemption from such abuse that I still can't forget it. It got their attention. I too wanted to tell them about a redeeming God who loved them, but how? I could relate to some of their fight, but definitely not all. I prayed that God would give me a message.

Toward the end of the week leading up to it, still not feeling God's direction about what to say, I frantically looked for a place to be alone. I found it in an empty bathroom in the back of the dark auditorium. I went into the stall with my Bible, praying and paging through until I came to the parable of the sower.

As I held the Bible close in the low light, I saw the first soil type in a way I never had before. Luke says, "As he was scattering the seed, some fell along the path; it was trampled on, and the birds ate it up" (Luke 8:5). The seeds along the road did not have a chance to burrow and grow in this soil. It was too hardened to accept it.

I gave Him heartfelt thanks right there on the throne.

I'd like to tell you I stood in front of those girls and spoke well. That's not how I remember it. But I did it. And covered the main points: God loves us. But sometimes people do not treat us with the love that God desires, and the hurt that happens can close our hearts. We harden to the point that it is difficult to let people in. Even a loving God who can be trusted, who desires to save and restore.

The girls were motivated to make things different for their children, I knew that. I may have said that when He comes in and heals your path, it changes the direction of the next generation too. I hope I said that.

Was a seed able to burrow a little bit that day for them? I don't know. But it did for me. He is faithful.

Father, thank You for Your touch that changes us.

THE MAKING OF A KING

The LORD is my shepherd.

PSALM 23:1 KJV

Saul had to be pulled from hiding to be crowned king, but twenty-five years later, he would stop at nothing to protect his throne, even killing the prophet of God who had anointed him. When God asked Samuel to anoint the king who would take Saul's place, He gave Saul a cover mission: Take a heifer to Bethlehem and say he was going to offer a sacrifice.

As soon as Samuel saw the teenage shepherd David, God identified him as the one, and Samuel broke out the anointing oil.

David had probably spent most of his life with the sheep. He was learning to be king as he came to see God as his shepherd, in the same fields that, one thousand years later, would witness angels announcing the birth of the Savior. David was growing in relationship with the One who would make him lie down in green pastures if he needed rest; who would lead him beside peaceful waters in a land where water was not that plentiful; whose tender touch restored even his soul. David came to identify the personal attention of God as Shepherd who would risk His life to rescue one.

But did he understand that Samuel's anointing meant that he was to be king? We do not know. In 1 Samuel 16, the prophet doesn't mention it. Perhaps because it would have endangered David's life.

Afterward, David went back to his day (and night) job. I imagine him sitting here, looking around, thinking, *Okay, so . . . I'll just stay here?*

But things started to happen almost immediately, including his slaying of the giant Goliath, which led to David being put in charge of the men of war. He was succeeding at whatever he did, and gaining public favor without even trying.

God was moving David into position to be king without him doing a thing to help. It would be fifteen years before that would happen, a long and often difficult journey, but each step on the path to the throne was his calling just as much as his eventual title of king. He believed that God would accomplish what concerned him (Psalm 138). He wasn't trying to reach his calling, but love the God who was so real to him.

Bible teacher Beth Moore said, "You'll never miss your calling if you're seeking the heart of God. Just be with Him. He'll send you out."

For many years I questioned my purpose, or even how God can love me. I venture there sometimes still, but my stays are getting shorter. He gives us the antidote for doubting in telling me, telling us, to draw near. As David did. Seeking His heart will lead us to Him, who gives fulfillment and purpose.

Jesus, I trust You that You are even now accomplishing what concerns me. I will take delight in You today, knowing You love me and won't let anything You have for me get away.

DISTORTION RACKET

He who abides in Me and I in him, he bears much fruit,
for apart from Me you can do nothing.

JOHN 15:5 NASB

Have you ever faced a task that scared you to death? When you thought, *there is no way I can accomplish this.* . . . Writing a book brought me there. I had to ask myself: Am I going to believe what God says through His Word and concentrate on that?

- That I have the mind of Christ (1 Corinthians 2:16).

- That God embodies power and soundness of mind, and He gives that to me (2 Timothy 1:7).
- That He is faithful, and He has called me into joint participation with His son Jesus (1 Corinthians 1:9).

Or am I going to fall into what I've always done in the past?

Okay, I thought. *God has been faithful in the past, but this was sooo far beyond me.* I looked at the calendar and got hot flashes. "I can't do this! You know I can't do this!" And then I felt His calm response: *Good. That's the starting point.*

We are not the sum total of our callings, or even our ability. His job is to accomplish, we just have to make sure we show up and believe that He is capable. We start moving forward when we get to the point of depending on Him.

If we look at yesterday in our "I can't" there'll be plenty of supporting evidence agreeing with us. The accuser will proof-text his message—he'll pull things from our past to try to prove that we can't do it. But if we are following God's purpose, even though it sometimes feels like walking into a fog, He'll provide what we need beyond our own capabilities. All we have to believe is that *He* is able.

These false beliefs about what we are capable of can also corner the market on our imagined responses to things that haven't happened yet. The picture we constantly show ourselves is often highly inaccurate. Those imagined responses don't know us at all. The responses we envision from others are also often dead wrong.

This is not a new strategy used by Satan against us. Two thousand years ago, Paul recognized it and pointed out a battle plan. "We are destroying speculations and every lofty thing raised up against the knowledge of God, and we are taking every thought captive to the obedience of Christ" (2 Corinthians 10:5 NASB). When we start to speculate and doubt, we need to take into account His power within us, because that trumps all.

When I abide in Him, when I spend time training myself in His Word and in prayer, I will bear much fruit. *We* will bear much fruit in our journeys toward the One "who is able to do far more abundantly beyond all that we ask or think, according to the power that works within us" (Ephesians 3:20).

I will push forward, even in my inability and my insecurity, in *anticipation* of His faithfulness. We are not stuck where we are or always have been. He can be trusted.

Father, You are trustworthy.
Thank You for making all things new.

THE GOODNESS OF GOD

The LORD is good to all;
he has compassion on all he has made.

PSALM 145:9 NIV

My dad never talked about any of his grandparents until I was an adult, when he made one comment about his grandfather not being a nice guy—he once forced his son, who had a broken hand, to saddle a horse. It's the only thing I know about him. I wish I knew more.

If someone reads only the parts of the Bible that talk of God's judgments, they will likely walk away with faulty conclusions about God. David, whose long relationship with God started when he was just a boy, wrote: "Your gentleness makes me great" (Psalm 18:35 NASB).

The judgments of God usually came down after many warnings and over a long period of time to people He desired to draw close to Himself.

God started His people from scratch, calling out one man, Abraham, from his father's house, giving him direction, protection, favor. If God would have withheld His intervention in any one of these areas, would the nation have come about? He gave a promise of blessing to Abraham. Including a far-reaching one: "In you, all the families of the earth will be blessed" (Genesis 12:3). This was to become the lineage of Jesus.

We do not have to go beyond that chapter in Genesis where God first called Abraham to see that this man was not perfect. His wife Sarah ends up one of Pharoah's wives because Abraham takes direction from his fear and says that she is his sister. When God struck Pharoah's household with great plagues, He also somehow communicated the reason to Pharoah, who confronted Abraham: "Why did you say, 'She is my sister,' so that I took her for my wife? Now then, here is your wife, take her and go" (Genesis 12:18–19).

God didn't change His mind about Abraham and send him away. He continued to direct, protect, and favor Abraham. Judgments came on the nation hundreds of years later, after their history had become a chronicle of failure to follow God. He wanted their love for Him to produce faithfulness, trust, and obedience. But they worshipped the gods of the nations around them, whose land the Lord had given them. Whose practices included temple prostitution and child sacrifice.

God is the same yesterday, today, and forever. The God who knew and protected Abraham is the same God who knows and protects me. Like my knowledge of my grandpa, I don't yet know the whole story, but I want to. I am learning His laws as well as His goodness.

The God who takes one man by the hand to build him into a great nation with far-reaching blessing, holds out His hand to individuals today for His specific purposes and specific blessings.

Do we believe that about Him?

Father, thank You for Your goodness that is
beyond comprehension. Help me to see through
the "good for me" part of Your love
to the goodness of Your heart.

ISLANDLESS

You are the body of Christ,
and each one of you is a part of it.

1 CORINTHIANS 12:27 NIV

The expression "No man is an island" has been written into song lyrics, books, stories, and on the fabric of culture for years. Do you know where it comes from? A devotional, written in 1624 by John Donne.

Devotional books have been around for a long time, and for good reason: We gain from the insight and experience of others in their walk with God. *The Imitation of Christ* was written in the early 1400s, about the same time as the invention of the printing press. Good timing. The devotional had over 700 reprints before the mid-1600s! It remains high on the most-translated-books list.

The truth is, we gain something of God from others that we can't see by ourselves.

Hebrews 11 gives a short history of those with strong trust in God. The last two verses of that chapter summarize, "These were all commended for their faith, yet none of them received what had been promised, since God had planned something better for us so that only together with us would they be made perfect" (NIV).

Then, chapter 12 leads us into the "therefore." We take courage from their stories, to run this race with our eyes on Jesus.

We see this connectedness throughout the Bible. After Jesus revealed Himself to Saul in a bright light on the road to Damascus, Saul sat for three days blind. Then God told Ananias to go and pray for him, and "something like scales fell from his eyes" (Acts 9:18 HCSB). Why the temporary blindness? And why send Ananias?

Saul was a Pharisee, descended from Pharisees (Acts 23:6). His identity was in keeping the law, in being separate. Did Jesus send Ananias to show Saul that it was no longer about *being separate*, but *doing together* in Him? That He brings people with different gifts and purposes together to accomplish His will?

I used to pray with a woman who was a friend of my

sister. When she and I both moved out of state to the same small town, we became friends. One day in the middle of the prayer, her head popped up, eyes wide. "I just had a vision of you!"

Now, I am not one who has ever seen a vision, and they were not a part of my church background. But when she explained the simple picture she had been given, I knew immediately what it meant. It revealed something about me that I had not seen on my own. She didn't know it's meaning, but it opened a window to a stronghold in my life.

Paul describes believers as Jesus's body. His inspired words showed that we don't just share beliefs, we complete one another. It is not an exaggeration to say that my friend's vision of me was life changing.

He created us to interact. That looks different for different people, but everyone is needed. No one is an island.

Father, thank You for the picture of You
that I see through the lives of others, and the wholeness
that comes to us through You in them.

LONG SEASONS

> *You are my God . . . I will praise Your name,*
> *for You have accomplished wonders,*
> *plans formed long ago, with perfect faithfulness.*
>
> ISAIAH 25:1 HCSB

Near the end of her life, my grandmother spent most of her time in bed, but one Sunday afternoon we pushed her wheelchair to the dining room table, her oxygen tube trailed back across the house to her bedroom. Surrounded by the noise of a big family gathering, she softly spoke her last sentence. "You think it's going to last forever."

She didn't repeat it when asked, or answer any questions. Some speculated that she was talking about the flowers on the table. She was soon falling asleep, and we wheeled her back to her bedroom.

My grandmother's last words echo Billy Graham's answer when asked about his greatest surprise about life. "The brevity of it," he responded without hesitation. "Time moves so quickly, and no matter who we are or what we have done, the time will come when our lives will be over."

I think the surprise comes after so many seasons that seem to last forever. My grandmother raised enough children that they slept more than two per bed. I'm sure there were years when it seemed like she left the laundry room only for the kitchen.

Do we trust God with our future when we seem stuck in one season, or the chaos level is high and it seems like no one is in charge? For me, the answer is not always. But the more I spend time seeking to know God better, the more I see that He wants me to trust in His goodness toward me.

God's faithfulness isn't contingent on anything inside us, isn't that amazing? He answers our helpless requests, even for the ability to trust Him for a future not yet seen.

When we're following His will, we're moving forward in His purpose for us even when it seems like we're standing still. The endless steps of today take us to tomorrow. My grandmother trusted in God, and He was there for her, finding room even next to that mile-high pile of dirty laundry. I'm so thankful for her example of sacrificial love.

We can remain steady on the path that's under us, even in the confining mundane, because He's right there with us, with perfect faithfulness and plans formed long ago.

Lord Jesus, don't let me get anesthetized into thinking
life is random or unending. My place in history,
the people I go through life with, and what touches
my life are all pieces that You gently weave into
the masterpiece of me. On the days when life seems
really long, help me to remember how purposefully
You planned where I am right now.

REVEALED

Peter went up on the housetop about the sixth hour
to pray. And he became hungry and wanted something
to eat, but while they were preparing it,
he fell into a trance and saw the heavens opened
and something like a great sheet descending,
being let down by its four corners upon the earth.

ACTS 10:9–11 ESV

It's rare that we can see the full scope of God's plan, especially from just one point in time. In Acts 10 we see that God chose to work through two different visions from two different people to bring about a revelation that shocked the Jewish believers and forever changed the world.

While waiting for a meal to be prepared, Peter saw a vision of a sheet coming down out of heaven with an assortment of unclean animals. A voice came to him, "Rise, Peter; kill and eat." Peter declines. "By no means, Lord; for I have never eaten anything that is common or unclean." The voice replied: "What God has made clean, do not call common."

This happens three times before the sheet is pulled back up to heaven. In his confusion, Peter hears the Spirit speak. But instead of telling him what the dream meant, He informs Peter that three men are looking for him, and to go with them without question.

The men were sent by Cornelius, a God-fearing Roman military commander, who was directed by an angel in a dream to send for Peter. Peter went with them the next day.

When he got there and saw all the people who had assembled to hear him, he thought he then knew the meaning of the vision. "God has shown me that I should not call any person common or unclean," he said. Jewish people did not normally associate with Gentiles, even enter their homes. Then Peter asked Cornelius the reason he had sent for him and Cornelius tells of his own vision four days prior, of a man in bright clothing who said: "Cornelius, your prayer has been heard and your alms have been remembered before God. . . ."

Then Peter realizes the full meaning of the vision he'd had. When Jesus had told them to go out into all the world, it wasn't just to God's chosen nation scattered abroad. The thousand-year-old foundation of their spiritual identity had shifted. There were new sheep for the fold.

While Peter is still telling them of Jesus's crucifixion as payment for their sin, and resurrection giving the gift of eternal life, the Holy Spirit came down on them. Peter and the Jews who had come with him were amazed.

The Holy Spirit could have just told Peter, "There is now no partiality." Instead He spoke to two different people who didn't know each other and were 40 miles apart to weave together a mosaic of His masterpiece for creation: acceptance to *all* who believe.

Each of us plays a part in a bigger plan and purpose that only God can see. Our time here—at this place, maybe with people we haven't even met—is part of a bigger picture that God has orchestrated long ago. God says His plans for those who love Him are beyond what we ever imagined.

Jesus, thank You for how You mysteriously orchestrate people and plans for Your good purpose.
Help us to trust You for the part that You have given to us.

STILLNESS

The LORD is good to those who depend on him,
to those who search for him.
So it is good to wait quietly for salvation from the LORD.
And it is good for people to submit at an early age
to the yoke of his discipline:
Let them sit alone in silence beneath the LORD's demands.

LAMENTATIONS 3:25–28 NLT

I read recently that crying is a healthy connection of body and soul; it is a physical response to what your soul is feeling.

If that is true, Jeremiah was a healthy guy. He wrote: "Oh that my . . . eyes [were] a fountain of tears, that I might weep day and night" (Jeremiah 9:1 NASB). For forty years, he poured himself into warning his nation of God's impending judgment, urging them to turn away from Baal worship and stand faithful to the Lord God. He had chosen them, He desired to shower them with prosperity in return for their faithfulness.

But not only did Jeremiah's fellow countrymen not listen to him, they hated him. He stood in contrast to the false prophets who promised a bright future.

Jeremiah wrote the book of Lamentations after all his unheeded warnings came true. Jerusalem was laid waste: People were slaughtered, the temple destroyed, captives taken. The book pours out like a funeral dirge. Yet, right in the middle of it, a ray of light breaks through.

This I recall to my mind, therefore I have hope.
The LORD's lovingkindnesses indeed never cease,
for His compassions never fail, they are new every
morning; great is Your faithfulness (Lamentations
3:20–24 NASB).

With everything literally having fallen down around him, hope springs up in Jeremiah, because he knew something about God: His lovingkindness, His compassion, and His faithfulness *do not stop*, despite how things look.

In the verses that follow, Jeremiah references his "yoke." I believe this yoke was the self-discipline of waiting for the Lord, which is repeated often in those verses. God makes Himself known to us, too, in the waiting. The Amplified Bible of verse 28 reflects God's good intention: "Let him sit alone [in hope] and keep quiet, because God has laid it on him [for his benefit]."

God had called Jeremiah to be His prophet long before he was even in his mother's womb (Jeremiah 1:5). Isn't that amazing? Can we believe that the God who gave Jeremiah the emotional makeup specifically designed for his purpose, has also specifically arranged who we are for ours?

When was the last time we accepted God's invitation to "be still and know that I am God"?

Thank You, Father, for who You are.
Give us the ability to sit quietly before You.

FIRST LOVE

That He would grant you, according to the riches
of His glory, to be strengthened with power through
His Spirit in the inner man, so that Christ may dwell
in your hearts through faith; and that you,
being rooted and grounded in love, may be able
to comprehend with all the saints what is the breadth
and length and height and depth, and to know
the love of Christ which surpasses knowledge,
that you may be filled up to all the fullness of God.

EPHESIANS 3:16–19 NASB

Throughout the Bible, we see God searching for a faithful love from His people. When it does not happen, when His people repeatedly embrace idol worship, the judgments predicted in the books of the prophets come. But those prophetic books include some of the most tender words in all of the Bible about God's all-consuming love and plans for our future and hope.

In Zephaniah, a three-chapter book that predicts a judgment called "The Day of the Lord," we see the intensity of God's delight in us. "The LORD your God is with you, the Mighty Warrior who saves. He will take great delight in you; in his love he will no longer rebuke you, but will rejoice over you with singing" (3:17 NIV).

Can you picture God rejoicing over you with singing? Amazing. Our one window into this awesome love is found in a book about punishment.

The *bent* of our God is restoration, bringing us back to that pre-sin walk in the garden, and a love that exceeds all other love.

In his letter to the Ephesian church, Paul's intricate prayer shows how dependent we are on God to understand His love:

- His strengthening enables Christ to dwell in our hearts.
- It provides a stable root system that supports an understanding we couldn't have on our own of the full dimensions of His love.

- Not just how tall and how wide it is—but His love is a three-dimensional love that enables us to enter in, surpassing our own knowledge.
- This knowledge is a prerequisite to "all the fullness of God."

Who would have been bold enough to pray for the fullness of God if it had not first been in Scripture? God wants all His fullness for us! In return, He asks for our first love. It's non-negotiable.

What does this mean for us? God wants us to love Him with all the strength and passion we have, despite what is going on in our world. He simply wants us to love Him like we love no other so He can fill us up with "all the fullness of God."

Father, thank You for Your enabling all the way.
Please fill us with Your fullness.

ON THE ALERT

Be of sober spirit, be on the alert. Your adversary,
the devil, prowls around like a roaring lion,
seeking someone to devour.

1 PETER 5:8 NASB

When I was a senior in high school, I met a girl a few years older than me who had a love for all things outrageous. Her creativity, compassion, humor, bear hugs, and so many other things were like a breath of fresh air. She was a gift from God, so needed at that time in my life.

She told me crazy things about her life before she met Jesus. About how when she was a child, she saw her grandfather standing outside her house, describing in detail to her mother what he had been wearing. Her grandfather had died before she was born. How she had out-of-body experiences, and saw both a fatal car accident and a murder as they were taking place. About her car driving on its own to the house of a known witch in our hometown. And about how she was able to read minds, but couldn't once she came inside the doors of our church.

After I graduated from high school, we had sporadic contact, but would pick up where we left off anytime we connected. She eventually moved out of state, and as the years passed, didn't respond often to my Facebook messages.

I was visiting home when I heard news about her that I didn't want to believe. I drove to her brother's house, and he confirmed: She had committed suicide.

Her mother said that she had been diagnosed with mental health issues, and could not find the right medication. I asked her about the out-of-body experiences my friend had told me about. She confirmed the stories and gave more detail.

A few months before she died, my friend said she could feel evil forces coming against her. She had become a recluse. It was a rare comment that I heard from a mutual friend after her memorial service.

Author C. S. Lewis said, "There are two equal and opposite errors into which our race can fall about the devils. One is to disbelieve in their existence. The other is to believe, and to feel an excessive and unhealthy interest in them."

There are some people who can go their whole lives and never encounter that Satan is real and active. It seems to me that he targets certain people for harassment. My sister believes he targets those who have a special prophetic anointing from God.

There is so much I don't know about what happened inside my friend. But this I do know: Satan is a roaring lion, working 24/7 to kill, steal, and destroy. His strategy is fine-tuned to our individual weaknesses, and isolating us makes his accusations more believable.

I also know that Jesus is more powerful. His love overcomes, pulling down strongholds, calling us by name to redeem, honor, and restore.

Being on the alert against Satan includes not opening the door to evil by playing with anything that has spiritual power apart from God. Everything good comes from Him, including life, and a future of hope and purpose. To believe anything else is to fall prey to the enemy.

Thank You, Father, for Your incredible power
and plan of goodness for us.

HIS BANNER OVER ME

The sons of Israel shall camp, each by his own standard,
with the banners of their fathers' households;
they shall camp around the tent of meeting at a distance.

NUMBERS 2:2 NASB

At every sporting event in the United States, we sing the "Star Spangled Banner," written by Francis Scott Key during a nighttime battle in the war of 1812. He wrote of watching for the flag reflected in the light of bombs against the night sky, taking courage in seeing the banner still waving over the land of the free and the home of the brave. That representation of their identity against the dark sky meant victory.

God first identified the Israelites as "my people" when He called Moses as their deliverer. They had gone into Egypt as the extended family of Jacob, or Israel, and God brought them out with the identity of His own. They obviously did not have a flag for national identity, but they did have banners, or standards, that identified each tribe, the twelve sons of Jacob and their descendants. Banners signaled where the Israelites should set up camp—in a specific order around the tent of meeting—and they lead the way on the journey. There were also military banners, which served as rallying points.

The Israelites won their first battle in the wilderness after God empowered them by a type of banner. Moses had stood on a hill over the battle with his staff raised. With the staff up, the Israelites led. When his arm came down, their enemies led. With help from two faithful supporters, he held it up for the duration.

After the victory, Moses built an altar and named it "The Lord is My Banner." It is not clear if this referred to the staff Moses had lifted, or if Moses was referring to God's instruction to him to "Write this in a book as a memorial and recite it to Joshua, that I will utterly blot out the memory of Amalek from under heaven" (Exodus 17:14). Both reflected a remembrance of God.

But the Hebrew soldiers, who had left Egypt as slaves, had witnessed the Red Sea move out of their way when

Moses raised his staff. Seeing that staff raised high would be a sign of victory to them.

In Psalm 60, David wrote, "You have given a banner to those who fear You, that it may be displayed because of the truth. That Your beloved may be delivered" (verses 4–5).

God sets His identifying, rallying banner of truth over us: We are His. It is for us to look at as much as our enemies, proclaiming: Look! Identified! He will deliver me, His beloved.

That banner is His Word, it is our strength and identity. "I have redeemed you; I have called you by name; you are Mine!" (Isaiah 43:1). Believing, speaking, and memorizing His Word will transform our identity.

His Word is our victory, no matter how dark the night sky. Let's continually look to that.

Father, thank You for Your banner of truth
that calls me Your own.

MORE OF HIM

*While My glory is passing by . . . I will put you
in the cleft of the rock and cover you with My hand
until I have passed by. Then I will take My hand away
and you shall see My back.*

EXODUS 33:22–23 NASB

Moses spent more one-on-one time with God than any man. His name was often on the lips of Jesus and the religious leaders of Jesus's day. But when God first introduced Himself to an eighty-year-old Moses as the God of his father, and Abraham, Isaac, and Jacob, Moses responded by hiding his face in fear.

"Come, I will send you to Pharaoh that you may bring my people, the children of Israel, out of Egypt" (Exodus 3:10 ESV). Forty years prior, Moses had tried to defend one of his people against their oppressor and ended up killing an Egyptian. God was calling him to a purpose and passion that had been buried by the years. But Moses wasn't there now.

"Who am I?" Moses asked.

God responded to Moses's identity question with a promise of His presence. "Certainly, I will be with you." And a sign: After Moses has brought the people out to that mountain, he would worship God there.

When Moses asks God what he should say if the Israelites ask his name, He said, "I AM WHO I AM." Which could be translated, "I will always be who I have always been." (*New American Standard Bible*: Charles F. Stanley Life Principles Bible Notes).

God gave Moses a detailed script: what to say and how people would respond. He previewed for Moses two of the miracles He would perform through him. Moses's doubt continued. "I am not eloquent. . . . I am slow of speech and tongue." Again God answered not by addressing Moses's abilities, but His own: "Who has made man's mouth? . . . I will be Your mouth and teach You what to say."

Finally, Moses flat out asked God to send someone else. Even though angry, God gave him the help of his brother

Aaron, saying, "Is there not your brother Aaron the Levite? I know that he speaks fluently." (A little sarcasm?)

By the time Moses had gone into Egypt, spoken for God during the plagues, led the Israelites through the Red Sea, and experienced his people's distrust of Him, his attitude toward God looked much different. Moses only wanted more:

> "If you are pleased with me, teach me your ways so I may know you and continue to find favor with you. . . ."
>
> The LORD replied, "My Presence will go with you, and I will give you rest."
>
> Then Moses said to him, "If Your presence does not go with us, do not send us up from here. . . ."
>
> And the LORD said to Moses, "I will do the very thing you have asked, because I am pleased with you and I know you by name."
>
> Then Moses said, "Now show me your glory." (Exodus 33:13–15, 17–18 NIV)

A face that had hidden from God was now asking to see something of Him than was humanly impossible. And God became actively involved to make that happen: putting Moses in a cleft in a rock, covering him with His hand, removing His hand to reveal Himself from behind.

Moses's fear was replaced by a fearless capability in His presence, and a desired intimacy that was returned by God as He made their relationship legendary.

Where are we in our relationship with Him: the first mountaintop experience, hiding; or the second, desperate to know Him more? We sometimes hide, or do the bare minimum, when there are things in our life that aren't pleasing to Him. But when we turn toward Him, the identity that our far-from-God mindset tried to pin on Him falls away as we experience His full, uncondemning acceptance and love.

Father, thank You for figuring out a way to show us Your glory.
Give us a hunger and thirst to know You more.

IN LOVE?

Jesus replied, "All who love me will do what I say.
My Father will love them, and we will come
and make our home with each of them."

JOHN 14:23 NLT

I came across a blog post recently whose comments actually made it through my computer's filter. It was written by a Christian, an opinion piece that sparked several hundred responses and a lot of strong opinions. It was fun to read. The author was diligent to respond, and polite. But her response to someone's comment, "God is in love with you," stopped me. The author thanked her for saying that, but said she preferred to simply think that God loved her.

Why would she want to draw that line?

I can understand a reluctance to frame God's love in human relationship language. It could imply that it's not necessarily long-lived. Maybe. But any little preposition that wants to pitch in and help us understand a love that is beyond comprehension is worth at least considering, don't you think?

Of course, the Bible often compares a marriage relationship with our relationship with God. "For this reason a man shall leave his father and mother and shall be joined to his wife, and the two shall become one flesh. This mystery is great; but I am speaking with reference to Christ and the church" (Ephesians 5:31–32 NASB).

But sometimes we *can* assign God faulty human characteristics without realizing it.

When we say "used by God," we mean God has directed someone or something in His will and for His purpose. In other context, when we say someone was "used" by someone else, it refers to selfishness. Taking from someone at their expense. We know God doesn't do that. God *gave* at His expense. Yet there have been times when I've realized that I was trying to give God a reason to answer my prayers for people. Like He needed a motive.

Sometimes we put other qualifiers on what God will be willing to do. Catherine Marshall wrote:

When [Jesus] wrapped a towel around his waist, poured water into a basin, and began to wash his disciples' feet (see John 13:4–5), Simon Peter objected that this was beneath the dignity of the Master. . . . But Jesus answered him, "If I do not wash you, you have no part in me." This is a stunning and stupendous thought. Unless I believe in this much love for me, unless I can and will accept him with faith as my servant as well as my God, unless I truly know that it's my good he seeks, not his glory (He already has all of that he can use for all eternity), then I cannot have his companionship.

It is truly my good He seeks, not His glory? Doesn't there have to be something in it for Him?

I think my gauge of what there has to be for Him, along with our language about His love, will always fall short of the reality of Him. He is able to love us like there is only one of us to love. He is in it for us, not for Himself. Not selfish, selfless. He is actively in love with us.

Jesus, please help me to love like You do.

SHAMELESS

I pray God your whole spirit and soul
and body be preserved blameless.

1 THESSALONIANS 5:23 KJV

In his devotional, *My Utmost for His Highest*, Oswald Chambers explores "your whole spirit" from the verse above: "The great mystical work of the Holy Spirit is in the dim regions of our personality which we cannot get at. . . . There are motives I cannot trace, dreams I cannot get at—my God, search me out."

This came to my mind after listening to a Bible teaching recently on YouTube. The text was the woman with the "issue of blood" from the Gospels. According to Levitical law, she was unclean and everything that touched her was unclean. She came up behind Jesus "because she thought, 'If I just touch his clothes, I will be healed'" (Mark 5:28 NIV).

I hadn't thought too much about her unclean status before then. How everything that touched her was also unclean. I had read the story many times and never had the reaction I did that night. It connected with something inside me; I wasn't sure why.

As I listened, and started journaling, it became clear.

For the first time, I was seeing her from behind. For over a decade, she had lived as someone no one "clean" wanted to touch. If they had known the truth about her, no one would have wanted to come near. But her belief drove her to Jesus. It quietly pulled up along the curb, and she hopped out and snuck up the back. She didn't want to be seen or heard, which was good. No one was facing in her direction anyway. No one saw the twelve long years that she had lived with her shame. No one felt the hands that had been trained to heal taking her hope and all her money.

She maneuvered through the crowd until she was at just the right spot, then thrust her hand forward to connect with Jesus. What treatment after treatment couldn't do, her faith in reaching out and taking hold of Jesus accomplished on the spot.

But He wasn't about to let her slip away. He stopped, and the entourage did with Him. "Who touched me?" He didn't have to ask. She was already healed. He was on His way to heal a child. When He refused to continue on, she fell at His feet and confessed everything.

"Daughter, your faith has healed you. Go in peace," He said (verse 34).

To a woman who had lived for so long as untouchable, Jesus insisted on eye contact. He wanted to see her, speak to her, and send her away in peace, her shame exposed and released.

We serve a God who sees the whole of us, everything unclean, everything faithful. And His focus on us drives home what His sacrifice accomplished: We are perfect in His sight, without shame or blame.

Father, thank You for what You endured for me,
and Your embracing acceptance.
Help me to show others what You have shown me.

NO VENEER HERE

God is spirit, and those who worship Him
must worship in spirit and truth.

JOHN 4:24 NASB

I read recently that ancient cultures like the Romans, Egyptians, and Mesopotamians handed down one-sided versions of their histories. "Examples of defeat are astonishingly absent from their wartime chronicles," according to *The Case for Christ Study Bible*. Even their kings were near perfect.

The multiple authors that God called to write His Word have this in common: honesty. God doesn't do pretense. The accounts in the Bible were not whitewashed, including every detail in the lives of His chosen people. The Bible shows a clear picture of our need for Him.

If Jesus had left heaven to enter creation and be born into a poor family, that would have been amazing enough. But He was born in a stable. Is it accurate to say He wasn't concerned with appearances? I think He was concerned. God orchestrated His Son to be born in the humblest of circumstances. The shepherds witnessed the night sky light up with angels issuing His birth announcement, mentioning His location in the trough, and praising God. *Glory to God in the Highest. And on earth peace among men with whom He is pleased.* The glory of the Truth offered no place for shame.

In a way, we *are* His trough, His manger, my sister has said. "He was wrapped in swaddling clothes and laid in a rough hewn, wooden manger to demonstrate that He was not put off by our lowly, raw, messy and dirty condition. His love for us compelled Him right down into the middle of our mess and it is from the center of it—of us—that He heals, cleanses and begins to redeem us. His place inside us takes us from brokenness to beauty."

Jesus said that taking care of the least influential in society was like taking care of Him. He stepped down from His throne in heaven to associate with those who were least likely to try to pretend to be good. And consistently called out those who polished their outsides only and were quick to condemn the sins of others.

When we can see ourselves for what we are, in need of a savior, and accept that forgiveness, the pretense is unnecessary. We are become like Jesus, perfect, holy and dearly loved by our heavenly Father (2 Corinthians 5:21; Colossians 3:12).

Father, thank You for requiring our authenticity,
and the treasure You see in us.

OUR EXAMPLE

Let no one look down on your youthfulness, but rather . . .
show yourself an example of those who believe.

1 TIMOTHY 4:12 NASB

After I had given a two-week notice at a former job, my boss took me out to eat to say good-bye. During lunch, we talked about the transition out of high school. She said that is a time when kids have to find their own faith.

That struck me as wrong, but at the time I wasn't sure how. Now I know. While post-high school is a great season when we can define or redefine ourselves, faith doesn't start at the doorway of adulthood.

David was called as a boy, chosen over all his older brothers because even then, He had a heart established after God's own. On the sheep fields, he'd experienced Him through a day-by-day relationship that led to trust, which put all the adult soldiers to shame when he faced Goliath. David wasn't finding his faith, he was facing giants with it.

The Bible shows time and again that God doesn't look at a person's age as a qualifier for His purposes. God called the prophet Samuel when he was too young to know what God sounded like, and the little boy thought the priest Eli was calling him (1 Samuel 3).

I've heard that Mary, the mother of Jesus, was as young as twelve or thirteen when the angel visited, as that was a culturally acceptable time of engagement. After one question of how, she showed great trust. "Behold, the bond-slave of the Lord; may it be done to me according to your word" (Luke 1:38).

Paul wrote to Timothy, a young pastor, to not let anyone look down on him because he was young, but show himself an example in all the hardest areas: speech, conduct, love, faith, and purity. Timothy could not control how others looked at him, but he could control his actions, and Paul had the utmost faith that others would see Christ in him.

I saw a picture posted on Facebook of a teenager kneeling down by a homeless man who was sleeping. The person who took the photo said they thought the kid was there to steal from the man. As they watched, they saw that he put his hand on him, bowed his head, and prayed over him. Yes, I shared that.

What an example to all of us.

Thank you, Lord, for the younger generation,
who so often show us what real faith looks like.

IF YOU . . .

Gideon said to God, "If you will save Israel
by my hand as you have promised—
look, I will place a wool fleece on the threshing floor.

JUDGES 6:36–37 NIV

I once applied for a writing job, was brought in for an interview, and botched it. I walked out to my car rolling my eyes. My head may have been twitching. I didn't bother to send a follow-up thank you. I imagined him laughing as he threw it away. But a week later I did send him an article I had written, with a note that said even if I didn't work in-house, I would like to freelance. He published the article. An editor on the inside told me that he was impressed with it. I didn't hear from him about that job, but saw that he hired someone who was right out of college.

Later, when they advertised for an editor, I really wanted to apply. What could it hurt? So what if I don't get this job either? That is what my mind was telling me. Everything else in me was saying, *Heck no. I won't show my face there again.* I told God that if He wanted me to apply, please have the guy I interviewed with come up behind me somewhere in town. It was a small town. There were only three grocery stores. It wasn't impossible. I gave God that crack in the door and eventually forgot about it.

I don't remember how long it was afterward that I was parked along a city street, and his car pulled up behind mine. I was envisioning this happening in a store, so I didn't even realize that my prayer had been answered until a few days later.

I'd like to say that I followed through, like Gideon did. When God called him to deliver Israel from the Midianites, he asked first that God would show him a sign that he would be successful. He asked that God would see that a piece of sheep's wool left out overnight be wet with dew in the morning, but the ground around it dry. When it happened, Gideon asked God for the opposite: that the ground be full of dew and the wool dry the next morning. When God answered him again, Gideon was all in. Even when God had Gideon *downsize* the Israelite army to only

300 men, Gideon followed God's plan unquestioningly. And God won the battle for them by confusing the enemy army until they then killed each other.

I wish I could have a do-over with how I responded with my own *If You . . . Then I* prayer. I reasoned myself out of applying: It had been too long. The job wasn't posted anymore. Was that really God's answer anyway? Blah.

If I ever offer a prayer like that again, I'm ready to do a Gideon and run with the faithfulness that God reveals.

Lord, thank You for Your trustworthiness
even when mine falters. Your continued love
makes me raring for another opportunity
to make You proud.

IDENTIFIED

*But, of course, there must be divisions among you
so that you who have God's approval will be recognized!*

1 CORINTHIANS 11:19 NLT

There were two conversations that I knew I needed to have. Both with people I love, but the topics were difficult and I just kept putting them off. One of them for months.

Why didn't I think sooner to ask Jesus, who blue-printed communication, to open the way for those conversations? After months of guilt and I-know-I-should shame, both happened unexpectedly and so naturally. I was able to speak with love and acceptance. Both ended well. A major victory for me. I was flat-on-my-face grateful.

When I was a teen, I memorized Ephesians 4:29: "Let no unwholesome talk come out of your mouths, but only what is helpful for building others up." The desire was there. The implementation, not so much.

It was something I struggled with for years. Abraham Lincoln is credited with saying, "Better to remain silent and be thought a fool than to speak and remove all doubt." Silence seemed my best strategy.

Decades later, when reading through the New Testament with a couple friends, 1 Corinthians 11:19 stopped me. I didn't remember ever seeing it. In it, Paul reveals an earmark of those with God's approval: how we handle division or differences of opinion. I saw myself clearly. My ugliest moments were when I disagreed with someone or someone disagreed with me. Sometimes it was just a strong opinion that caused me to slip into attack mode, often subtly (unless it was with my sisters). I definitely did not have God's seal of approval in that area.

Now, when I disagree with someone, I keep that realization from 1 Corinthians in front of me: How I react will identify who I serve. Is it myself?

Colossians 3:12 has helped show me how my interaction with others should be ordered. "Therefore, as God's chosen people, holy and dearly loved, clothe yourselves with compassion, kindness, humility, gentleness and patience" (NIV).

We need to soak in the first part for a while before getting out and "clothing" ourselves—we are chosen. We are holy. We are not just loved but dearly love. That is our identity and starting point. It flows from His heart, to ours, to others.

Father, thank You for Your love that brings us to You,
and desires us to call You Father. Let Your character
flow into us. Please guide me, especially when I disagree
with someone, or someone disagrees with me.
Let the words of my mouth and the meditations
of my heart be acceptable in Your sight.

STAND

Will you contend for Baal, or will you deliver him?
Whoever will plead for him will be put to death by morning.
If he is a god, let him contend for himself.

JUDGES 6:31 NASB

Once the Israelites reached the promised land, they were easily influenced by the nations around them. Nations whose land God had promised and provided His children would have seen the Israelites worshipping their gods, who had not delivered them. When God lifted His protection and allowed other nations to oppress them, they cried out to Almighty God and He sent a judge to deliver them. The book of Judges reads like a roller coaster of this falling away and returning. The leadership of the judges kept the nation from derailing.

God has often worked through the words of one individual who has had the courage to stand against the opinion that surrounded them. For example, when Gideon destroyed the altars of Baal, the men of Gideon's hometown demanded that Gideon's father, Joash, bring out his son so they could kill him. But Joash spoke up. His well-placed words turned the tide of public opinion.

Well placed words are so needed, and often remembered throughout history.

In 1774, when it was suggested that the first Continental Congress open with prayer, there was opposition due to a concern that the religious diversity represented was too great. Then one man, Samuel Adams, spoke up: He would support anyone of piety and character who was also a friend of his country. The next morning when the Congress opened, an Episcopalian clergyman read several prayers and Psalm 35.

John Adams described the results of the prayers in a letter to his wife: "I never saw a greater effect upon an audience. It seemed as if heaven had ordained the psalm to be read that morning." Adams said the clergyman then prayed spontaneously for America, Congress, Massachusetts Bay, and especially for Boston, that had recently been bombed. Adams reported that it filled the hearts of everyone, he'd never heard a better prayer, and begged his wife to read Psalm 35.

Have you ever spoken up like that? I am very good at it, when I am picturing it in my mind. In reality, there are many more times when I haven't spoken than times when I have. It isn't easy at all. But God enables, and He tells us not to worry about what we will say for those times. He tells us to trust and rely on His Holy Spirit.

He's the one who gives us courage to be that one person. The one voice of reason with life-changing results that could be remembered forever.

Father, thank You for the examples of those who have not been afraid to speak up. Thank You also for the voices that history has not yet heard.

LETTING GO

*When she could hide him no longer, she got him
a wicker basket and covered it over with tar and pitch.
Then she put the child into it and set it among the reeds
by the bank of the Nile. His sister stood at a distance
to find out what would happen to him.*

EXODUS 2:3–4 NASB

What was Moses's mother thinking as she tarred and pitched the basket that would take her baby from her? Had the Lord given her a mysterious hope that it would somehow be her baby's salvation and not his final resting place?

There was no lack of suffering for anyone on her street. The Israelites had been in Egypt for over 300 years before

Moses was born, most of the time as slaves. In fear of their increasing number Pharaoh had instituted forced labor, but the more the Israelites were afflicted, the more they multiplied. When his plan to have the Hebrew midwives kill all the male babies didn't work, Pharaoh resorted to a direct command to the people: Every son born was to be cast into the Nile.

She could do nothing to save him but send him away. I wonder how long she lingered by the bank of the Nile before letting it go. It is a desperate feeling when we are powerless to hold close the ones we love the most.

But we can soak up the testimonies of others who have lived through it, and give testimony of a loving God in control. He sweeps in to comfort as only the Creator of our souls can, and gently takes the pieces in His hands.

The Pharaoh's daughter had come down to the river to bathe and noticed the basket. Moses's life was spared and he started toward a purpose God had planned long ago. Which included a short time back in the arms of the woman who had let him go.

God will redeem our loss. He is there in the chaos that comes with it, holding the pieces, whispering His presence and promises to work all things together for good. His compassions are without end, and are just as strong for you as they were for Moses's mother.

Father, thank You that we can trust You
in situations that we can't control,
and fall on You with hurt we can't handle.
Thank You for that promise of tomorrow,
and Your strength that carries us.

WHO YOU REALLY ARE

*The Lord . . . will bring to light the things now hidden
in darkness and will disclose the purposes of the heart.
Then each one will receive his commendation from God.*

1 CORINTHIANS 4:5 ESV

Author Bob Goff says, "The best way to show people that
God is everything we say He is—is for us to be everything
He says we are."

But how do we do we get there? Our adversary is constantly trying to get us to take dictation about who we are.
About how much power we don't have. About our lack of
significance in life. We can only recognize that dictation
by pulling close to God. We cannot discern that this voice

in our head isn't our own without Him. Isolating ourselves from others makes it worse.

He tries to dictate about our misplaced motives, our lack of commitment, our phoniness. While bad motives, lack of commitment, and inauthenticity happens, the foundation of who are is not there. It is in Christ, who dwells in our hearts in faith, who gives us the ability to understand the full dimensions of God's love.

It is His power within us that overcomes. "Now to him who is able to do far more abundantly than all that we ask or think, according to the power at work within us, to him be the glory I the church and in Christ Jesus throughout all generations" (Ephesians 3:20–21 ESV).

Actions are the language that helps reprogram our thoughts away from the lies we've listened to. Our actions communicate a truth to our spirits about who we are. So we can maintain our reflection when we walk away from the mirror. "But the one who looks into the perfect law, the law of liberty, and perseveres, being no hearer who forgets but a doer who acts, he will be blessed in his doing" (James 1:25).

Even if we have fallen down over and over, it does not mean that we are hypocrites, that deep down, we really don't love God. We continue on in this journey, not letting what is already done derail us.

First Samuel 12:20–21 says, "Do not be afraid; you

have done all this evil. Yet do not turn aside from following the LORD, but serve the LORD with all your heart. And do not turn aside after empty things that cannot profit or deliver, for they are empty."

Let's not let the shame of our past take us to places of more emptiness. Our doubt, our past absorption with self-destructive enticements does not change His desire for us, His kindness and love.

We understand who we really are by listening to the One who knows us. By coming to God unmasked and real. Henri Nouwen put it best:

> Prayer, then, is listening to that voice—to the One who calls you the Beloved. It is to constantly go back to the truth of who we are and claim it for ourselves. I'm not what I do. I'm not what people say about me. I'm not what I have. . . . My life is rooted in my spiritual identity. Whatever we do, we have to go back regularly to that place of core identity.

Thank You, Father, for Your incredible power that works within us, and Your great love that defines us.

ABOUT THE AUTHOR

J. K. Olson started out as a newspaper reporter before turning to freelance writing and editing. She and her husband have been married for twenty-four years and have three children.

IF YOU ENJOYED THIS BOOK, WILL YOU CONSIDER SHARING THE MESSAGE WITH OTHERS?

Mention the book in a blog post or through Facebook, Twitter, Pinterest, or upload a picture through Instagram.

Recommend this book to those in your small group, book club, workplace, and classes.

Head over to facebook.com/worthypublishing, "LIKE" the page, and post a comment as to what you enjoyed the most.

Tweet "I recommend reading #IrreplaceableYou by J. K. Olson // @worthypub"

Pick up a copy for someone you know who would be challenged and encouraged by this message.

Write a book review online.

Visit us at worthypublishing.com

twitter.com/worthypub

worthypub.tumblr.com

facebook.com/worthypublishing

pinterest.com/worthypub

instagram.com/worthypub

youtube.com/worthypublishing